C000162742

RANDOM
ACTS OF
POLITENESS

RANDOM ACTS OF POLITENESS

Eccentric, Quirky and

Occasionally Suicidal

Examples of Selflessness

and Courtesy

ANDREW TAYLOR

For Sam, Abi and Bec
Lucy, Sophie and Tom

Cover illustrations: spine: line art drawing of a girl curtseying (Pearson Scott Foreman, Wikimedia Commons); back, bottom: line art drawing of footballers (Pearson Scott Foreman, Wikimedia Commons); top: line art drawing of minuet dance (Pearson Scott Foreman, Wikimedia Commons).

First published 2011

The History Press
The Mill, Brimscombe Port
Stroud, Gloucestershire, GL5 2QG
www.thehistorypress.co.uk

© Andrew Taylor, 2011

The right of Andrew Taylor to be identified as the Author
of this work has been asserted in accordance with the
Copyrights, Designs and Patents Act 1988.

British Library Cataloguing in Publication Data.
A catalogue record for this book is available from the British Library.

ISBN 978 0 7524 5977 6

Typesetting and origination by The History Press
Printed in Great Britain
Manufacturing managed by Jellyfish Print Solutions Ltd

CONTENTS

INTRODUCTION

Everybody knows, of course, that standards of good manners have declined in recent years. Like the sunnier summers that we used to enjoy, the better music, the funnier jokes and the tastier dinners, this collapse of courtesy becomes increasingly obvious the older and more crotchety we get.

Plenty of the anecdotes in this book seem to support that view. They demonstrate the kindness, consideration and often courage that has been shown in the past by great generals and by ordinary soldiers, by kings and commoners, by people in high society and by very young children.

However, perhaps inconveniently, others will show that precisely the same qualities exist today. By Premiership footballers and international sportsmen, by journalists and television personalities, by the queen herself and from a simple teenage girl writing to her dad: there are contemporary examples of generosity, fellow-feeling, tolerance and decency that stand comparison with anything in the past.

The stories are true, and they come from a wide variety of sources, from our own age and from ancient history. Good manners and courtesy, they say, are not a matter of using the right fork to eat your devilled kidneys, and not much to do with remembering to say 'Please' and 'Thank you'; they are about treating people with unselfishness, sympathy and open-heartedness. Civilisation, perhaps, is a matter of treating people decently.

Often amusing, sometimes moving, occasionally astounding and always fascinating, *Random Acts of Politeness* is both a marvellous read and a tribute to some of the finest, if often overlooked, qualities of humankind.

Here, then, is a celebration of everything that is most noble and selfless in human beings – even if, just occasionally, the reader may be left thinking, 'These people must be barking mad!'

I

SOLDIER, SOLDIER

In the eighteenth century, it must often have seemed as if a degree of lunacy was a necessary prerequisite for success as a military commander. Certainly King George II thought so: told by some of his courtiers that General Wolfe, who had captured the Canadian city of Quebec from the French, was clearly mad, he is said to have retorted, 'Mad, is he? Well, I hope he will bite some of my other generals.'

But that apparent madness could result in exuberant displays of leadership and occasional blistering, reckless bravery and determination. It was an age of aristocratic panache, of extravagant gestures, of brash self-confidence, and of gentlemanly imperturbability under fire.

Perhaps those days are gone: soldiers, after all, no longer march off to war in the bright red uniforms that once made them such a tempting target for enemy riflemen; they no longer fight in smartly drawn-up square formations, firing off regular volleys of musket shot. But the military character has always valued courage, discipline and the readiness to sacrifice oneself for the wider good.

The idea of politeness and *savoir faire* in battle, when groups of men are straining every sinew in an effort to kill each other, may seem grotesque. But many of these stories demonstrate how aristocrats and commanders and ordinary footsoldiers, sailors and airmen alike, throughout history, have shown their true colours and their essential humanity under almost unimaginable pressure.

Some of them may seem barely sane; some show astonishing courage and self-sacrifice; some speak of sensitivity, even gentleness. But they are all stories about the way people can respond to the challenges of war and the danger of imminent death with grace, dignity and courtesy.

After you ...

The Battle of Fontenoy was fought on 11 May 1745, in present-day Belgium, as part of the War of the Austrian Succession. It may be largely forgotten today that it was a French victory over a combined Anglo-Dutch-Hanoverian force, but it is remembered for a bizarre exchange between two rival commanders.

Lord Charles Hay, commanding a detachment of the 1st Foot Guards (now the Grenadier Guards), marched his men to within musket shot of the French *Maison du Roi*, an elite regiment of the royal guards of King Louis XV. Since muskets – although they inflicted terrible injuries – were notoriously inaccurate, that meant they were barely thirty paces from the enemy.

Riding out in front of his troops, Lord Charles raised a silver hip flask towards the French in a mocking toast. *'Messeiurs les Gardes Françaises, s'il vous plaît tirez le premier!'* he called out ('Gentlemen of the French Guard, please fire first!'). One sergeant, staring at the levelled muskets of the French, is reported to have said: 'For what we are about to receive, may the Lord make us truly thankful!' But the French commander, the Comte d'Auteroche, was equal to Lord Charles' sangfroid.

'Gentlemen, we never fire first. Fire yourselves,' he replied dismissively, in perfect English. For a moment, it looked as though the battle might be postponed indefinitely, in a crazy ritual of 'After you – no, after you'. It is not certain who did actually fire first, although one account suggests, maybe unconvincingly, that the French loosed off a volley before the English had 'done laughing' at their sergeant's prayer for divine assistance. What is certain is that Lord Charles' guards subsequently fixed bayonets in a businesslike charge of the French lines which dislodged them from their position.

By the time the battle finished, at around two o' clock – just in time for a little late lunch for the aristocratic commanders – a total of some 15,000 soldiers had been killed. But whatever the precise truth of the story, the very fact it was so popular and repeated so often demonstrates what a gentlemanly business warfare was believed to be in the eighteenth century.

Facing the conquerors

King Christian X of Denmark was known for his habit of taking a morning ride without bodyguards through the streets of Copenhagen, during which his subjects were free to approach him.

These rides continued even after the Nazi occupation of the country, and the elderly King Christian mounted his own silent protest against the occupiers by publicly ignoring them. A long and fulsome telegram from Adolf Hitler congratulating him on his seventy-second birthday in 1942 received the dismissive reply: '*Meinen besten Dank, Chr. Rex*' ('My thanks, King Christian') – a slight that led to the recall of the German ambassador from Copenhagen and the expulsion of the Danish ambassador from Germany.

There were even stories that the king had responded to a German threat to force Danish Jews to wear a yellow star on their clothing by volunteering to wear one himself. There were no Danish Jews and gentiles in Copenhagen – only Danes.

Although the king's popularity angered senior German officers, they knew that any mistreatment of him might cause widespread trouble among the people.

In another well-documented incident, word was brought to King Christian that the swastika was flying over Christiansborg, the home of the Danish Rigsdag, or parliament. He immediately ordered that it should be taken down and replaced with the Danish flag.

This was done, but within hours, the German commandant had ordered that the swastika, the mark of German domination and Danish defeat, should be hoisted again on the palace flagpole.

King Christian telephoned him, and told him that if this were done, then a Danish soldier would be ordered to remove it again. In that case, said the commandant, the soldier would be shot by the German guards. 'I think not,' King Christian said. 'I will be that soldier.'

The swastika never flew above the Rigsdag.

Courteous, considerate & kind

The most dreadful of wars often start, at least, with a commitment to human decency, restraint and honourable behaviour. The horrific reality of trench warfare was still in the future when Lord Kitchener, Britain's Secretary of State for War, sent this message individually to each of the soldiers leaving for France in the British Expeditionary Force in August 1914: 'You are ordered abroad as a soldier of the king to help our French comrades against the invasion of a common enemy. You have to perform a task which will need your courage, your energy, your patience.' It said:

Remember that the honour of the British Army depends on your individual conduct. It will be your duty not only to set an example of discipline and perfect steadiness under fire but also to maintain the most friendly relations with those whom you are helping in this struggle. The operations in which you are engaged will, for the most part, take place in a friendly country, and you can do your own country no better service than in showing yourself in France and Belgium in the true character of a British soldier.

Be invariably courteous, considerate and kind. Never do anything likely to injure or destroy property, and always look upon looting as a disgraceful act. You are sure to meet a welcome and to be trusted; your conduct must justify that welcome and that trust.

Your duty cannot be done unless your health is sound. So keep constantly on your guard against any excesses. In this new experience you may find temptations both in wine and women. You must entirely resist both temptations, and, while treating all women with perfect courtesy, you should avoid any intimacy.

Do your duty bravely. Fear God. Honour the King.

Nearly ninety years later, in another war on another continent – almost in another world – Lieutenant Colonel Tim Collins used very different language to convey much the same message to around 800 men of the Royal Irish Regiment as they waited to cross the border in the allied invasion of Iraq in March 2003. Speaking off the cuff, without notes, he urged them to respect the Iraqi people:

We go to liberate, not to conquer. We will not fly our flags in their country. We are entering Iraq to free a people and the only flag which will be flown in that ancient land is their own. Show respect for them.

Don't treat them as refugees, for they are in their own country. Their children will be poor; in years to come they will know that the light of liberation in their lives was brought by you.

If there are casualties of war then remember that when they woke up and got dressed in the morning they did not plan to die this day. Allow them dignity in death. Bury them properly and mark their graves … If you harm the regiment or its history by over-enthusiasm in killing or in cowardice, know it is your family who will suffer. You will be shunned unless your conduct is of the highest – for your deeds will follow you down through history. We will bring shame on neither our uniform or our nation.

Our sons as well

Among the thousands of tributes all over Britain to the dead of two world wars are one or two that stand out because they extend their grief to former enemies. At Wareham in Dorset, the bodies of German soldiers, sailors and airmen of the Second World War – some of them washed ashore and others those of prisoners from nearby prisoner-of-war camps – lie in graves that are mingled among those of the British dead.

And in a village churchyard in Suffolk can be found a memorial to the crew of a zeppelin airship that crashed nearby during the Second World War. A few minutes before the crash, the crew could have been dropping bombs on the people beneath – but after burying them, the villagers had the following passage from the Bible inscribed in their memory: 'Who art thou that judgest another man's servant? To his own master he standeth or falleth.'

But perhaps the most generous tribute of all came after the terrible fighting between Allied and Turkish troops for the Gallipoli Peninsula during the First World War in 1915–16, which cost the lives of hundreds of thousands of men on both sides. Many were buried where they fell, and after the Allied retreat there was great anguish among the families of those who had died over how their graves would be treated by the Turks – particularly because stories of the alleged barbaric actions of both German and Turkish troops were commonplace in wartime Britain.

In fact, the graves were treated with honour, and after the war the bodies were re-interred in either Turkish or Commonwealth War Commission cemeteries, which are still beautifully tended to this day.

Turkey's Prime Minister, Mustafa Kemal Atatürk, who had commanded a Turkish infantry division during the fighting for Gallipoli, caused a memorial to be erected on the peninsula, on which were inscribed words generously addressed to the mothers of the fallen Allied soldiers: 'You, the mothers who sent their sons from faraway countries, wipe away your tears. Your sons are now lying in our bosom, and are at peace. After having lost their lives on this land, they are our sons as well.'

Few former enemies can ever have paid such a chivalrous, dignified and moving tribute to those against whom they had once fought.

A battle won

A good general never panics – and neither does a gentleman, as this story demonstrates. Lord Uxbridge led the charge of the heavy cavalry of the Royal Scots Greys at the Battle of Waterloo, taking more than 3,000 French prisoners. Later in the day, he was sitting on his horse next to the Duke of Wellington, watching the final stages of the battle, when a stray cannonball screamed through the air between them.

Uxbridge glanced down. 'By God, sir, I've lost my leg!' he exclaimed.

'By God, sir, so you have!' replied the duke.

The exchange was immortalised by Thomas Hardy in *The Dynasts*, his epic drama of the Napoleonic Wars. Hardy has Wellington, sitting astride his horse Copenhagen, going on to say:

Ay – the wind o' the shot
Blew past the withers of my Copenhagen
Like the foul sweeping of a witch's broom.
Aha! They are giving way!

The aristocratic insouciance which this story demonstrates, incidentally, did not mean that Wellington had no sense of the bloodshed and suffering that were the price of victory. In a sombre letter home after the battle, he observed sadly: 'My heart is broken by the terrible loss I have sustained in my old friends and companions and my poor soldiers. Believe me, nothing except a battle lost can be half so melancholy as a battle won.'

An affair of honour

For many years, the military authorities had an ambiguous attitude towards duelling. On the one hand, it exemplified the military virtues of courage and elan – but on the other, it was an extraordinarily wasteful way of getting rid of young officers.

As commander of the Allied armies in the peninsula and then in France during the Napoleonic Wars of 1803–15, the Duke of Wellington ordered that any of his officers who were involved in a duel would be severely punished. Nonetheless, in March 1829, by which time Wellington had become prime minister, he challenged another Tory politician, the Earl of Winchelsea, to a duel over a slight to his honour.

The quarrel had its origin in Wellington's promotion of Catholic emancipation. Winchelsea, who vigorously opposed improving the constitutional position of Roman Catholics, wrote to several newspapers accusing Wellington of treachery. His honour impugned, and despite his views on duelling, Wellington called Winchelsea out. The duel took place on Battersea Fields, London (now Battersea Park), a popular site for these 'affairs of honour', on 21 March. At the word the two men, armed with pistols, moved apart, then turned and faced each other at a distance of twelve paces to fire their single shot. Wellington fired, and missed. Winchelsea then 'deloped', deliberately firing his weapon in the air rather than take advantage of his now defenceless adversary. Honour was satisfied and the quarrel declared over.

Wellington later claimed that he had fired at Winchelsea's legs, to wound rather than kill him; since he was a notoriously poor shot, however, and was just as likely to have hit a vital spot, the other man was probably luckier than he knew. King's College, University of London, founded in 1829 by non-Anglican Christians and followers of other faiths, still celebrates 'Duel Day' on 21 March each year.

It has to be said that Winchelsea's graceful act in sparing the Great Duke when he had him at his mercy was perhaps at least as wise as it was selfless. Duelling was in any case illegal by that time, and to have killed or wounded the man who was not only prime minister, but also the greatest commander in British history and a popular hero as well, could easily have led to the earl being torn to pieces by a mob.

In fact, the whole custom of duelling has always been hedged around with courtesies and formalities, which have occasionally been used by those who have more shrewdness than courage to avoid a fight that they seemed likely to lose.

A century before Wellington, Sir William Petty, who served under Oliver Cromwell as a surveyor in Ireland, was challenged to a duel because of some real or imagined slight. Sir William was a man of many talents – doctor, mathematician, statistician and political economist – but he was not a fighter, and since his challenger was an officer with long and bloody experience in Cromwell's army, it seemed likely that he would come off second best. Worse, Petty was known to be extremely short-sighted.

However, since he was the one being challenged, he was entitled to choose where the duel was to be fought and what weapons should be used. For the place, he chose a pitch-dark cellar, and the weapons, carpenter's axes. His ingenuity brought the whole challenge into public ridicule, and so the duel – doubtless to Sir William's considerable relief – was cancelled.

A noble gesture made in vain

In March 1199, as he laid siege to the French town of Chalus, the great Richard Coeur de Lion – Richard the Lionheart – was wounded by a crossbow bolt shot from the walls by a young townsman. He went to his tent to try to pull it out, but eventually had to call in a surgeon who, according to the ancient chroniclers, made such a mess of the job that the wound became infected and gangrenous. By the time the town fell, the king was close to death.

He ordered that the young man who had shot him – named Bertrand de Gourdon in some of the chronicles – should be brought before him. 'What harm have I ever done you, that you should want to kill me?' he asked.

Bertrand, apparently unafraid of the king, his soldiers or the terrible punishments that probably lay in store for him, answered defiantly that his father and two of his brothers had been killed by Richard. 'Do what you will,' he said. 'I will die happy, if I can be sure that I have ridded the world of a tyrant who has defiled it with blood and slaughter' – not the most tactful speech for a man in his position, perhaps, but Richard was impressed with his spirit. He ordered that he should be set free, and gave him a hundred marks to help him on his way. It was a final noble gesture of chivalry by a king who was more often feared for his brutality in the field than praised for his magnanimity.

As a sad little footnote to this story of royal restraint and generosity, however, it is worth reporting that King Richard's gesture did Bertrand little good. As soon as the king was dead his military commander, the Provencal mercenary Mercadier seized the money for himself and had the young man flayed alive.

A chivalrous commander

The classical chroniclers Livy and Plutarch tell the story of a schoolteacher in the Etruscan town of Falerii in 394 BC,

which was being besieged by the Roman dictator Camillus.
He used to take the young boys in his care – the sons of
some of the town's leading citizens – for walks outside
the town walls. Day by day he took them a little further
from the town, persuading them each time that there was
nothing to fear, until eventually he led them in among the
outposts of Camillus' army and demanded to be taken to
the Roman leader.

Hoping to win the general's favour, and a large reward,
the schoolteacher declared that he had brought the boys to
him so that the city would surrender.

Camillus, however, was shocked. 'Even war has laws
which good and brave men will respect,' he said. 'We must
not pursue victory so ardently that we do not recoil from
the gifts of shameful and ungodly men. I am a great general
who will rely on my own courage to wage war, not on the
baseness of other people.'

Then, showing that he had a sense of humour to match
his sense of honour, he ordered that the schoolmaster
should be stripped naked, and the boys be given whips and
sticks so that they might drive him back into the city.

Sometimes, even in battle, virtue can be its own reward.
The people of Falerii were so impressed by a general
who valued justice more highly than conquest that they
surrendered. The chroniclers don't say what they did with
the schoolmaster.

Sauce for the goose

Restraint is not the most notable military virtue – few fights are won by pulling punches. But just sometimes, a military commander can enjoy the great satisfaction of holding back and allowing his enemy to dig a hole for himself.

The story is told of the exchange between the German and French delegations as negotiations got under way for the Armistice of 1919. The commander of the French forces, Marshal Foch, read out a list of conditions. The Germans were appalled. 'These are terms upon which no civilised nation could insist,' exclaimed one of the German generals.

'They are indeed,' replied Foch quietly and courteously. 'These are not the French terms today. These are the terms which the German commander imposed on the city of Lille when it surrendered.'

The wreck of the *Birkenhead*

HMS *Birkenhead* was an iron-hulled 210ft paddle steamer which was used as a troopship by the Royal Navy in the mid-nineteenth century. In February 1852 she made a brief refuelling stop at Simonstown in South Africa, after the long trip from Cork. On board were 132 ship's officers and crew, and some 480 soldiers from several different regiments, bound for the Frontier War that was being waged against Xhosa tribesmen in the Eastern Cape. With them were twenty women and children and several cavalry horses.

Early in the morning of 26 February, about half a mile off the ominously named Danger Point, near Cape Town, the ship struck a submerged rock and started to sink almost at once. Scores of men were drowned in their bunks – and when the crew tried to launch the lifeboats, they discovered that only three were serviceable. The bolts securing the rest were immoveable with rust and paint.

As the sailors struggled to free the boats, the soldiers stood in line on the tossing deck, awaiting orders as if they were on the parade ground. Some manned the pumps, some threw the horses overboard to try and swim for the shore, and others joined the fruitless struggle to launch more boats.

The rest – many of them little more than boys who had been in the army for only a few months – stood silently in their ranks, as though waiting for an inspection. Soon after the women and children had been helped into the boats and rowed away, the ship began to break up.

At this point, the *Birkenhead*'s captain shouted that all the men who could swim should try to make for the boats, but Lieutenant-Colonel Alexander Seton of the 74th Highlanders, the soldiers' commanding officer, realised that there was the danger that the boats would be swamped if they did so. He gave the order to stand firm, and the women and children watched as the soldiers, still without panicking or losing their discipline, were thrown into the sea as the ship sank in less than twenty minutes. Those who could swim tried to make for the shore, but few of them made it. Almost all were accounted for by cold and exhaustion, by the heavy seas, which pounded them against the rocks, and by the Great White sharks – later named Tommy Sharks after the soldiers or 'Tommies' who died.

Over 430 soldiers and sailors died in the shipwreck, including Lieutenant-Colonel Seton and the ship's captain, Robert Salmond; only 193 were saved. But among them were all the women and children; the discipline, courage and chivalry of the men on board, accepting almost certain death to give their loved ones the chance of survival, had not been in vain.

At the time of the *Birkenhead* disaster, the Royal Navy had no pre-planned emergency drill; it was the example of that day that led to the cry of 'Women and children first', the so-called '*Birkenhead* drill', which became the tradition in abandoning ship. Rudyard Kipling's poem *Soldier an' Sailor Too*, written more than forty years later, captured the lasting popular emotion about the *Birkenhead* story with his line: 'To stand an' be still to the *Birken'ead* drill, is a damn' tough bullet to chew.'

But perhaps the best tribute came in the direct, unemotional words of one of the survivors to the court martial that followed the disaster:

The order and regularity that prevailed on board, from the moment the ship struck till she totally disappeared, far exceeded anything that I had thought could be affected by the best discipline; and it is the more to be

wondered at seeing that most of the soldiers were but a
short time in the service.

The remains of the *Birkenhead* still lie in about thirty metres
of water, where she sank – a hidden, silent, but intensely
evocative memorial to a story of true heroism and military
discipline.

Hero or villain?

Andy McNab, the best-selling author and former member
of the Special Air Services, says that soldiers – special forces
soldiers, at least – never talk about 'the enemy'. Instead, they
use the neutral term 'players'.

It's an acceptance that, in most conflicts, both sides are doing
much the same thing: if the soldiers on one side had happened
to be born somewhere else, then they might have been
fighting in a different army. They may have more in common
with the men they are fighting than modern politicians, and
maybe even senior officers, might like to admit.

It's a professional attitude towards war that avoids blowing
bugles and waving flags, and it's one that has been prevalent
for centuries, not just with soldiers but sometimes with the
kings who used to command them as well.

An eighteenth century collection of anecdotes, the
Pocket Remembrancer of 1775, tells the story of a French king
taken to see the monument at Rouen to the memory of

England's Duke of Bedford. The French have no reason to remember the fifteenth century duke with any affection; as regent for the young Henry VI he rampaged through their countryside, defeated their armies, raped and pillaged in their towns and villages, and finally had their national hero, Joan of Arc, burned at the stake.

Bearing all this in mind, suggested one of the courtiers of the French king as he gazed on the monument, it might be a good idea to have the whole thing torn stone from stone to try to forget about a particularly painful period of French history.

The king – sadly the *Pocket Remembrancer* does not say which king it was – pondered for a moment. 'By no means,' he said finally. 'Let us not dare to disturb the ashes of a man who when he was living made all France tremble.'

Within a few years of the *Pocket Remembrancer*'s publication, of course, the French Revolution had swept away much more than just a monument to a long-dead foreign warrior. Today only a modern inscription in Rouen Cathedral notes that the Duke of Bedford ever existed at all – but the story of the respect and generosity of an unknown French king still remains. Andy McNab would probably approve.

A gesture of loyalty

In 334 BC, Alexander the Great was about to embark on the invasion of Asia which would lead to the destruction of the

Persian Empire and spread Greek civilisation as far as the foothills of the Himalayas.

He was determined that his generals should be able to leave their families well provided for while they campaigned with him – partly, no doubt, so that he could be sure of their loyalty and continuing commitment to his cause – and so he made grants to each of them of estates, villages and other property that would provide an income while they were away.

When he had nearly completed this distribution of most of the lands he possessed in Macedonia, his friend and loyal general Perdiccas asked whether he was keeping anything back for himself. 'I have my hopes,' said Alexander.

'Then we, your companions, will share in your hopes,' replied Perdiccas, refusing the land that Alexander was offering him. Several other generals did the same, preferring to show their loyalty to Alexander and his whole enterprise than to take possession of his lands before they had even set off.

A 'verray parfit, gentil knighte'

The Elizabethans valued courtesy as highly as courage – and knew that the two were often closely related.

Sir Philip Sidney, poet, courtier and soldier, was held to be the model of knightly virtue – the epitome of what Chaucer referred to as 'a verray parfit, gentil knighte' – and his death at the age of 31, fighting against the Spanish at the Battle of Zutphen in the Netherlands, September 1586, was greeted with shock in Queen Elizabeth's court. Sir Philip had been wounded in the thigh, and died after nearly a month in agony as the wound became poisoned.

But the story of his heroism was told almost immediately: lying injured and in great pain on the battlefield, he had handed his water bottle to an ordinary soldier who was close to death, with the words, 'Thy necessity is yet greater than mine.' For the Elizabethans, and for every age since, it was the sort of behaviour that meant that his name would live forever – and more than 400 years later, his statue still stands in Zutphen, close to where he fell.

2

I'M A CELEBRITY, GET ME OUT OF HERE - PLEASE!

It may be hard to feel sorry for celebrities and 'personalities'. The glitzy characters who habitually pop up on television, on anything from *Big Brother* or *I'm a Celebrity* to the TV news, often don't make it easy for people to like them off screen. Television breeds self-importance, and self-importance is the enemy of courtesy.

Sometimes, bad behaviour can bring its own reward: there is a famous sequence of photographs that show a young Mick Jagger leaving a nightclub. In the first, he has just angrily spotted the photographer; the second shows him waving an angry finger in the photographer's direction, and in the third, he is striding purposefully towards him, apparently intent on inflicting punishment. In the fourth, he is stretched embarrassingly on his back in the road, clearly having come off second best.

But to be fair, celebrities from A-list to D-list often have a lot to put up with: constantly flashing cameras, occasionally rude and unwelcome questions, and all the pressures of life in the spotlight. And yet some of them manage, with random acts of courtesy, grace and dignity, to demonstrate that they have personalities that go beyond just being a personality.

Can I have your autograph?

A personal story to begin with. As a young boy in the 1960s, I was at Headingley for a cricket test match, and I had been diligently filling in a scorebook all day, as young boys do. Every detail of the play was there, spelled out in dots, lines, figures, names and w's to mark the wickets for anyone who could read it. Looking up from my labours, I saw the actor James Ellis – a star of one of my favourite television programmes, a police series called *Z Cars* – standing nearby watching the match.

Since *Z Cars* was even more of a passion than cricket, I went nervously up to him hoping for an autograph – but since I had, even at that young age, a modicum of street wisdom I didn't ask him straight away. Instead, reasoning that he probably hadn't been there for long, I held out my book towards him. 'Would you like to see the scorebook?' I asked, shyly.

He seemed pleased, and spent several minutes looking over what had happened. Eventually, when he handed back the book with a thank you and a smile, I guessed it was the right time. 'Could I have your autograph?' I asked.

'Come back at the end of play and you can. If I sign it for you now, I'll have to sign dozens of them,' he said. Slightly crestfallen, I took my book and went back to my seat and my scoring. Then, when play finished for the day, I went back hopefully to where I had left him – to find that he had gone. I couldn't believe it; after all, he'd *promised*. I told myself I understood why he didn't want to be pestered by autograph hunters, and why he'd slipped away – but I didn't. It was the first time I'd actually been told a direct lie by a grown up, and it hurt.

And then, a few days later, I was leafing idly through my scorebook – and there, on the next blank page, were those magic words: 'James Ellis, PC Lynch, Z Cars.' He must have scribbled them in while I wasn't looking – taking a chance on being spotted by any of the other small boys hanging around. He didn't need to do it, and he never knew how much it meant to a 12-year-old boy. But it wasn't a bad example of courtesy and thoughtfulness, and I've never forgotten it.

Would you care to sit down? And you? And you?

The essayist, novelist and poet G.K. Chesterton wrote well over a hundred books during a thirty-six year literary career.

As he grew older, his wit, his bumptious enthusiasm and his recognisability – he was an extremely fat man, with a pince-nez and a bristling moustache – made him a celebrity before the age of television.

His wit could be biting, and he neither asked nor gave quarter in any of his literary, social or theological quarrels – but he was passionate about courtesy, and had a lively sense of humour about himself, particularly about his large size. At one lecture in the 1930s he told his audience: 'Just the other day in the Underground, I enjoyed the pleasure of offering my seat to three ladies.'

Don't die of embarrassment

Some subjects are not mentioned in polite conversation, and some words are never used. This convention may avoid embarrassment, but it can also lead to confusion, and even to tragedy.

One story, told by the famous raconteur and wit Ned Sherrin in his book *In His Anecdotage*, is an example of the misunderstandings that can arise from excessive propriety. Queen Mary, the former Princess of Teck in the Kingdom of Württemberg, and wife of King George V, was a kindly and considerate woman, but she was known for her awesome regal formality and propriety. On one occasion, she noticed that her senior detective had been missing for several days, and asked an equerry whether he was sick.

In fact, the policeman was at home, enduring a severe case of piles. Uncomfortable, embarrassing and making it difficult to sit down, perhaps, but hardly life-threatening. Yet the equerry felt he could not pass such intimate and indelicate information on to Her Majesty, and simply mumbled that the detective was suffering from 'an unfortunate disease'. The queen, no doubt grateful for his discretion, nodded sympathetically and said nothing.

A few days later, King George spoke to a second palace official. 'What are we going to do about this detective?' he asked.

'Oh sir, he'll be back soon,' came the reply. 'He's only got an attack of piles.'

The king, relieved but slightly puzzled, paused for a moment. 'Some fool of an equerry told my wife he had syphilis,' he said.

But often, the consequences can be much more serious. Elizabeth Branwell, the maiden aunt of the Brontë sisters who helped their widowed father with their upbringing in the Yorkshire village of Haworth, died of exhaustion brought on by constipation. A Victorian gentlewoman of high morality and considerable sternness, who would have approved unreservedly of the equerry's reticence, she was far too well brought-up to tell the doctor what her trouble might be.

Doctors still occasionally struggle against such evasiveness. One friend of the author's, being treated for cancer, was urged by his consultant not to hesitate to ask any question or report any symptom, however awkward it may be to find the words.

'You may die from cancer, although we'll do all that we possibly can to see that you don't,' the doctor said. 'But it would be a great waste to die of embarrassment.'

He didn't, incidentally, thanks to the NHS, and survives to tell the story.

Health & safety

The BBC's human resources department is known throughout the corporation for its occasionally pernickety attitude towards health and safety. Cameramen who may one week be dodging bullets in Afghanistan sometimes complain that a few days later they may have to listen to official instructions about how to climb a ladder.

In 2007, the BBC correspondent Damien Grammaticus was sent to report on the disastrous floods in Bangladesh which killed hundreds of people and left millions more homeless. This unavoidably involved travelling around the flooded villages in the motorboats that were being used to rescue stranded villagers.

There were several complaints to the BBC that Grammaticus and his team were taking up spaces that could have been used by refugees – an issue that concerned the correspondent himself as well – but the decision was taken that it was important that the story and the pictures should reach the world at large. By taking the video footage and reporting on the disaster, the team could help to encourage international aid that would help even more victims of the floods.

Back in London, however, HR staff had noticed something else: Grammaticus had been seen on screen reporting from a moving boat without wearing a lifejacket. This was potentially a serious 'health and safety' offence, and questions were asked of his newsroom bosses.

It turned out that the BBC correspondent and his team had insisted that their safety equipment should be used by some of the refugees who were piled into their boats. He has never spoken publicly about this, and can't understand why anyone would be interested in the story.

Getting the message across

Many people believe they have better manners than they actually have – only a very few make the opposite mistake. The writer Evelyn Waugh, however, author of such well-loved classics as *Scoop* and *Brideshead Revisited*, was taken aback by a letter from his friend, the society beauty Lady Diana Cooper. In it, she said that her husband Duff Cooper had been surprised and grieved by a report he had heard that Waugh had detested him for more than twenty years.

'I am very sorry to hear that,' Waugh replied. 'I must have nicer manners than people normally credit me with.'

Or maybe not; one of Waugh's other remarks on the subject ought to be noted as well. 'Manners,' he once said, 'are especially the need of the plain. The pretty can get away with anything.'

A backhanded blessing

Sir William Davenant was a famous and highly respected poet and dramatist of the seventeenth century, who is now buried in Poet's Corner in Westminster Abbey. Apart from his literary efforts, his celebrity in his own day derived partly from his encouragement of the rumour that he was the illegitimate son of William Shakespeare – a rumour which, the gossip John Aubrey cruelly pointed out, gave his mother 'a very light report, whereby she was called a whore'.

Aubrey also recounts how he caught either gonorrhoea or syphilis from 'a black handsome wench that he lay in Axe Yard, Westminster', and, as a result, lost his nose.

Sir William was constantly being offended by the cruel jokes and ribaldry that his misfortune caused among the wits of literary London, so he was deeply touched by the courtesy of a simple old woman who saw him in the street, commented on his condition, and offered him her blessings on his eyesight.

'Why would you bless my eyes, woman?' he asked.

She explained that without a nose, should his eyesight begin to fail, there would be nowhere to balance a pair of spectacles.

Business tactics

The nineteenth-century French novelist Alexandre Dumas, *père*, author of *The Three Musketeers* and *The Count of Monte Cristo*, won fame first as a brilliantly successful playwright whose works could be guaranteed to fill any theatre in Paris.

One day, he was visited by the angry manager of one of the biggest theatres in the city, who stormed into Dumas' room in his hat and coat, and demanded to know if the rumour was true that Dumas' latest play had been sold to a smaller rival.

Indeed it was, said Dumas, and the theatre manager immediately made a huge bid of his own in return. It was much bigger than the other company's offer, and the manager had no doubt that Dumas would accept it without demur.

But the famous playwright shook his head. He would stand by the bargain he had made, he said, particularly because of the tactic that the representative of the smaller company had used to persuade him to sign the contract.

'And what was that?' the disappointed bidder asked.

Simple, said Dumas; 'When he spoke to me, he removed his hat.'

Death on the *Titanic*

Many myths and legends have gathered around the sinking of the *Titanic* in April 1912 – but one of the best authenticated is that of the courage and chivalry of Benjamin Guggenheim, the fabulously wealthy fifth son of the legendary mining magnate Meyer Guggenheim, and one of the biggest celebrities of his day.

The 46-year-old Benjamin had boarded the ship at Southampton for her maiden transatlantic voyage, along with his mistress, a French singer named Léontine Aubart, her maid Emma Sägesser, Guggenheim's valet Victor Giglio (with whom he shared a stateroom) and his chauffeur René Pernot.

After the liner struck an iceberg shortly before midnight on Sunday 14 April, Guggenheim and Giglio helped the two women into one of the lifeboats. It was nothing, Guggenheim reassured them in German, the ship only required a repair and would soon resume its voyage: 'We will soon see each other again!'

But it was clear by then that his optimism was ill-founded; with the lifeboat launched, he and Giglio returned to their stateroom, took off the lifejackets and heavy sweaters they had been wearing, and donned full evening dress. 'We have dressed in our best, and are prepared to go down like gentlemen,' one survivor remembered hearing him say. Another was given a message for Guggenheim's wife in New York. 'If anything should happen to me, tell her I've done my best in doing my duty,' he said.

Both he and Giglio perished, as did the chauffeur, whose second class cabin was in a different part of the ship. Léontine Aubart and Emma Sägesser survived to be rescued, however, and lived on into the 1960s, both dying in their late seventies.

A circumspect reply

Often, particularly when dealing with a vain and ageing film star, courtesy may amount to little more than intelligent self-interest. Who wants to upset a good client, when all you have to do to keep her sweet is swallow an obvious reply? You can, after all, tell the truth and still be courteous – and circumspect. Take this reported exchange between Marlene Dietrich and an anonymous photographer.

'Your photographs are not so good any more,' she told him. 'Eight years ago, you used to make me look wonderful.'

'Yes,' he replied, nodding sadly. 'But I was much younger then.'

Superstar

Modern performers sometimes seem to equate star quality with rudeness – but the late Sammy Davis Junior showed that it can often be something very similar to courtesy. Back in the 1960s, he was performing at a club in Lake Tahoe, Nevada, before a crowd of some 800 diners.

He opened with three of his old favourites, but well before he had reached the end of the third song, it was clear that he wasn't on top form. He stopped, thought for a moment, and then picked up the microphone again. 'Folks, some nights I can do it, and some nights I can't. I guess tonight, I can't,' he said, shaking his head regretfully. 'I'm really sorry to let you down, but I guess the least I can do is ask you all to be my guests.'

With that, he left the club – having first paid more than $17,000 for the food and drinks of the entire audience.

A modest composer

The German Romantic composer Johannes Brahms enjoyed a period of staggering popularity in the late nineteenth century, lionised across Europe both for his original compositions and for his skill as a conductor.

However, this adulation could not turn his head, and he remained a modest man who hated flattery. Two stories make the point.

He was invited to dinner by one of the greatest wine connoisseurs of Hamburg, his home town, and as the first bottle was poured, the host explained that it was the finest wine in his extensive cellar. 'This,' he told the assembled company, 'is the Johannes Brahms of my collection.'

As he watched anxiously, Brahms picked up his glass, swirled the wine around the bowl, and inhaled its delicate bouquet. Finally, he took a sip, and then put the glass down again without comment. After a moment or two, his anxious host could wait no more. 'How do you like it?' he asked nervously.

'Delicious, truly delicious, my friend,' replied Brahms. 'But I think I would like to try your Beethoven.'

On another occasion, in November 1881, Brahms attended an official dinner in the Hungarian capital, Budapest, after performing as soloist in the first performance of his own *Second Piano Concerto*. The work, which Brahms himself described as 'the long terror', is a challenge for any pianist, but is widely considered one of his most impressive compositions.

At the dinner, as the guests were being invited to drink a toast to 'Germany's most celebrated composer,' Brahms interrupted. 'Quite right – Gentlemen, here's to Mozart!' he said.

In fact, there was another finely judged expression of courtesy after Brahms performed the same piece sometime later, this time from one of the critics. There was no doubting the originality and power of the composition, but Brahms' own playing was little more than competent. The critic

Eduard Hanslick, a close friend of the composer and a fervent admirer of his work, wrote that Brahms now had more important things to do than to practise for hours each day.

After all, who would be the person to tell Johannes Brahms that his playing was not up to scratch?

An undeserved rebuff

Courtesy, of course, is not always repaid in kind. The American poet and anthologist Louis Untermeyer was once invited to speak to a small literary group, and accepted their offer of a fee for his efforts. When he attended their meeting, however, he saw for himself how limited their resources were, and generously returned the money to their treasurer, saying that he was sure that it could be put to a good use.

Meeting the man again sometime later, he inquired what 'good use' they had found for it. Slightly incautiously, the treasurer replied that it had been paid into a fund to get better speakers to address their meetings.

A most famous greeting

Few people have heard of John Rowlands, who was born into a poor Welsh family, grew up in the workhouse, and emigrated to the United States at the age of 18 to seek his fortune. There he was taken in by a wealthy merchant who gave him a job, a home and a new name, Henry Morton Stanley. The young man eventually forged a career for himself as a journalist, and was subsequently sent by the *New York Herald* to find out what had happened to the famous British explorer, Dr David Livingstone.

His book *How I Found Livingstone*, written some years later, describes the moment of his success in Ujiji, near Lake Tanganyika in present-day Tanzania. There in the jungle, the two men addressed each other with the stilted, slightly awkward courtesy of Victorian gentlemen, and Stanley uttered what has become probably the most famous greeting of all time:

As I advanced slowly towards him, I noticed he was pale, looked wearied, had a grey beard, wore a bluish cap with a faded gold band round it, had on a red-sleeved waistcoat and a pair of grey tweed trousers. I would have run to him, only I was a coward in the presence of such a mob, would have embraced him, only, he being an Englishman, I did not know how he would receive me. So I did what cowardice and false pride suggested was the best thing – walked deliberately up to him, took off my hat, and said, 'Dr. Livingstone, I presume?'

'Yes,' said he, with a kind smile, lifting his cap slightly.

I replace my hat on my head and he puts on his cap, and we both grasp hands, and I then say aloud, 'I thank God, Doctor, I have been permitted to see you'.

He answered, 'I feel thankful that I am here to welcome you'.

Generosity & sensitivity

By 1873 the French landscape painter Jean-Baptiste-Camille Corot enjoyed a glittering reputation among the connoisseurs and art dealers of Paris. His canvases sold for thousands of francs, and he was a wealthy man, known for the generosity of his donations to charities. He could also show remarkable sensitivity towards the feelings of those he tried to help.

He heard that the caricaturist, painter and sculptor Honoré Daumier, whose work he had admired for many years, was nearly blind, living in poverty and threatened with eviction from his cottage in the village of Valmondois because he could not afford to pay the rent.

Corot secretly bought him a house, and wrote to explain what he had done:

My old friend ... I have a little house at Valmondois for which I cannot think of a use. It occurred to me that I could give it to you, and since I like the idea, I have already registered it in your name. I'm not trying to do you a good turn – simply trying to annoy your landlord.

Daumier's reply was brief but heartfelt: 'You are the only man from whom I could accept such a gift without humiliation.' Afterwards, the two artists painted each other's portraits in the garden of Daumier's new home, and it was from there that he travelled to attend the first solo exhibition of his life, just a year before he died. Corot's generous and sensitive gesture had given him a few years of peace and simple comfort after a lifetime of struggle.

Correcting a mistake

It's not only conventionally nice people who are capable of sudden and instinctive acts of kindness, generosity and courtesy. The legendary motor magnate Henry Ford, for example, was known to be a ruthless bully in his private life, an anti-union despot in his factories and an early anti-Semitic supporter of Adolf Hitler – maybe not the first man you would turn to for charitable contributions.

But on a visit to Dublin – Ford was proud of his Irish roots, and tried to buy his ancestral home at Ballinascarty – he donated £2,000 towards the construction of a new orphanage. His gesture was spread all over the front of the next day's papers, but a careless reporter or an incompetent typesetter reported his gift as £20,000. Embarrassed, the director of the appeal went to Ford's hotel to apologise, and said he would phone the newspaper editor at once to insist that the mistake should be corrected.

'No need,' said Ford. 'Why don't I just give you the remaining £18,000 instead?' And he took out his cheque book at once and did just that.

A surprising donation

During the 1930s the Catholic Worker Movement ran a hostel for down-and-outs in New York. For many of them, it was their only refuge from life on the streets – but because it failed to meet the city's regulations, the organisation's founder, Dorothy Day, was fined $250.

On her way to pay the fine at New York's Manhattan Upper Court, she came upon a group of drunks and beggars gathered on a street corner, who were asking passers-by for money. She had almost passed them when one individual, indistinguishable from the rest, sidled forward and pressed a piece of paper into her hand. 'I read about your problems, lady, and I wanted to help. Here's two-fifty,' he mumbled, before drifting back into the crowd.

She thanked him as he disappeared: $2.50 would not go far towards paying the fine, but she was touched and delighted at this small gesture of support from what she assumed must have been one of the occupants of the hostel.

It was not until she had almost reached the court that she looked at what she had been given. It was not, as she had thought, a couple of banknotes, but a cheque. It was for $250, the full amount of her fine. And it was signed W.H. Auden.

She was sorry she hadn't recognised him, but it was understandable, as she said later, 'Poets do look a bit *unpressed*, don't they?'

Yet another rejection slip

Anyone who starts writing for a living knows what a rejection slip looks – and feels – like. By the time they've achieved success they've often forgotten. But a journalist who used to work with George Orwell on *Tribune* in the 1940s tells the story of how he found him, then the magazine's literary editor, stuffing something into a packet with a guilty look on his face.

One of the tasks which Orwell most disliked was sending back unaccepted submissions to their unlucky authors – and on this occasion, folding up the unusable verses that had been sent in along with the bland rejection slip, he was surreptitiously adding a 10s note of his own to the bundle. It was a small gesture, but it says much about Orwell and his feelings for the poor.

A strange invitation

There are many stories about William Archibald Spooner, Warden of New College, Oxford – most of them apocryphal.

His famous inability to get his words right – telling an undergraduate he had 'tasted a whole worm', for instance, rather than 'wasted a whole term', and looking for a pub called the Dull Man in Greenwich when he should have been in the Green Man in Dulwich – brought the word Spoonerism into the language.

But for all his occasional confusion – especially in his old age when he was warden, or head, of his college – he was a kindly and courteous gentleman. In his seventies, he was walking in the college quadrangle when he met a stranger about whom he could remember nothing except that he was a newly appointed Fellow.

'I'd like you to come to tea tomorrow,' he beamed. 'I'm giving a little party in my room for the new Mathematics Fellow.'

The stranger, a much younger man, looked slightly embarrassed and very anxious not to cause offence. 'But Warden,' he stammered, 'I *am* the new Mathematics Fellow.'

Spooner was not remotely put off his stride. 'Never mind,' he said. 'Come all the same.' And off he went.

A gentle awakening

The great Austrian classical pianist Artur Schnabel was known for his intellectual seriousness rather than his sense of humour; except for when he noticed one evening that an elderly woman in the front row of the audience at one of his recitals had fallen asleep.

As the audience applauded enthusiastically at the end of his performance, she suddenly jerked awake, and looked around guiltily. As the applause died away, Schnabel leant across to apologise. 'I'm sorry, madam, it was the clapping,' he said. 'I was playing as quietly as I can.'

The importance of a tie

Great artists and other celebrities may sometimes get away with ignoring the dress code that is suggested by their hosts – struggling up-and-coming writers, as the young Mark Twain found out, cannot.

Twain, his great novels still unwritten, was invited to the home of his neighbour, Mrs Harriet Beecher Stowe, in Hartford, Connecticut. Her anti-slavery novel, *Uncle Tom's Cabin*, had made her famous on both sides of the Atlantic, and she insisted on a proper deference. So when her guest, a genial and friendly man who often had little time for social formalities, turned up with his shirt collar undone, he was roundly upbraided by his hostess in front of all the other guests for not wearing a tie.

The next morning, a messenger arrived at the Stowes' front door, carrying a small parcel wrapped in brown paper. Inside was a black tie, and a note, which said: 'Here is a necktie. Please take it out and look at it. I believe I was with you for about half an hour without this necktie. At the end of that time, would you be good enough to return it, as it is the only one I have. Mark Twain.'

Jesse James or Robin Hood?

The American outlaw Jesse James terrorised the American West in the aftermath of the Civil War, shooting and killing bank employees and anyone else who got in his way, while at the same time assiduously burnishing his image as a Robin Hood figure who stole from the rich to give to the poor.

While he certainly earned the first part of that reputation, there is little evidence that he ever did much giving, either to the poor or anyone else. But scores of stories grew up about him, many of them describing his courtesy and elan.

One tells of an elderly widow at whose house the James gang stayed while they were on the run from the law. She had no idea that they were outlaws, and opened her heart to them, describing her struggle against poverty since the death of her husband and telling them how hard she was finding it to manage. The very next day, she said, a debt collector was coming to collect $1,400 which she owed to the bank – and since she had no money to give him, she would be evicted from her farm.

As the gang left the next morning, James handed her a packet. Inside was $1,400 with which she could pay off her debt – the proceeds, although she didn't know it, of Jesse James' latest raid. Brushing aside her thanks, the outlaw reminded her to demand a proper receipt for the money, and rode off with his companions.

After a short distance, they stopped in a clump of trees close to the trail and watched the debt collector ride past on his way to the farm. Then a few minutes later, as he rode back down the trail to take the money he had collected back to the bank, they held him up at gunpoint and took back the $1,400.

They had the money and the widow had her receipt, so everyone – or almost everyone – was happy.

One word of praise

The great actor Henry Compton – said to be the finest performer of Shakespeare's comic roles in the nineteenth century – was once buttonholed by an aspiring colleague who unwisely asked him: 'Do you think my performance last night was good?'

Unfortunately it hadn't been, but Compton didn't want to hurt his feelings. 'Good?' he asked enthusiastically. '*Good*, my dear chap? Good isn't the word …'

3

HOME IS WHERE ...

With our own families and in the privacy of our own homes, surely, we can act as we please. Many people, once they have closed the front door behind them, behave in ways that would make them ashamed in public. Home, perhaps, is where you hang your head – or at least, where you would if you thought for a moment about your behaviour.

But there's no reason why we should treat friends, work colleagues, and even complete strangers with courtesy and consideration, and then forget about the people closest to us. The stories in this chapter show how people have dealt with some of the problems we all face occasionally at home and in our daily lives. Sometimes they've got it wrong; sometimes they've ended up looking foolish – but they've generally had the very best of intentions.

A twinkle in his eye

It can sometimes be difficult to separate courtesy from affection. Maybe, in fact, the gentle demonstration of feeling is the truest courtesy between two people who are very close.

The Arabian traveller, poet and writer Charles Doughty, the author of the classic *Travels in Arabia Deserta*, could behave like a cantankerous old man even in his thirties – at the age of 35 he would point to his long beard and demand the respect to which he said he believed his great age entitled him. As he grew older he was not one to forget a slight or lay aside a grudge and he would bury himself in his books for days at a time, leaving his wife Caroline and their two daughters to look after themselves.

And yet, after forty years of marriage, he still treated Caroline with courtesy, affection and respect. Towards the end of his life, he would search out some newly budding flower in the garden and bring it inside for her, hiding it behind his back with a twinkle in his eye, and make her guess what it was that he had found.

He never realised, his daughters said later, that Caroline, who did all the gardening, had watched as all the flowers grew, and knew better than he did what was in bloom. So as he was doing his best to treat her with kindness by showing his affection with these spur-of-the-moment little gifts, she was returning the compliment by playing along with the game and pretending to be surprised.

Different recipes for a happy marriage

English people have traditionally been uneasy with public displays of affection: showing too much emotion towards one person, it seems, might be considered discourteous towards everyone else. In William Congreve's comedy *The Way of the World*, written in 1700, Millament sums up how she thinks a marriage should be conducted:

> Don't let us be familiar or fond, nor kiss before folks, like my Lady Fadler and Sir Francis … Let us never visit together, nor go to a play together, but let us be very strange and well-bred. Let us be as strange as if we had been married a great while, and as well-bred as if we were not married at all.

Hardly a great recipe for a happy married life, then. And yet there are plenty of examples of people who have managed to remain impeccably well-bred, and still demonstrated their feelings quite openly. Being considerate towards the rest of the world, in other words, doesn't mean you have to be dismissive about the person you love.

For example, in the early 1940s the celebrated writer and caricaturist Sir Max Beerbohm, then in his seventies, was with his elderly wife at a party. A gaggle of young actresses and models were trying to catch his eye, all of them, as one guest said, 'painted … with the determination to gain attention'. It must have been a flattering experience for the old man. But Beerbohm looked at them and shuddered, then turned to his wife and said, 'My dear, you are looking so charming tonight that I simply must talk to you.'

I believe in you

It's not just the relationships between lovers or husbands and wives that call for honesty, openness and consideration. The football manager David Jones appeared in court in December 2000, then in charge at the Premiership club Southampton, charged with the sexual abuse of young boys at a special school where he had once worked. The charges were later dismissed out of hand, with the judge telling him: 'No wrongdoing whatsoever on your part has been established.' But on that morning, Jones – married for twenty-three years and the father of four children – was facing the destruction of his entire world.

Then his 16-year-old daughter, Chloe, handed him a card:

Dad,

I never say this to your face, so I'm telling you on paper how much I love you. I'm not the world's most perfect child and I'm at an age where I never show affection towards my parents, but you mean the world to me. I want to take away your pain, but I can't. The people accusing you are nothing, and you are everything. Stand up to them, Dad, and show them you are strong. They will never break you. I don't believe in God because I don't see how he can allow these things to happen to such a good man. But I do believe in hope and faith, and most of all I believe in YOU.

Love, Chloe.

Four days later, the prosecution case collapsed.

Saying the wrong thing

In your own home, your guard may be down. You may be relaxed, even careless – and the most generous, courteous and thoughtful gesture may be ruined by the wrong choice of words.

Take the man whose wife rang a radio programme to complain about the fact that he had been doing some ironing. From what she said, it was clear that until that morning he hadn't picked up an iron for several years.

So what was wrong with that? Many wives would be delighted to have a husband who does the ironing, even if only rarely. But that wasn't the point.

'It's what he said,' she complained. 'He handed me a pile of ironing that he'd finished and said, "There you are, I've ironed all my shirts for you."'

Don't mention it

It's often said that if you step on somebody's toe on the New York subway, the very least you can expect to receive is a torrent of abuse and invective – while if you do the same thing on the London Underground, your victim will probably apologise for carelessly putting his toe under your foot.

But even in England, few people can shrug off an injury with the same aplomb as the young Thomas Macaulay. At just 4 years old, the future Lord Macaulay – politician, poet and historian – was with his parents on a visit to Lady Waldegrave at Strawberry Hill, near Twickenham, when a careless servant spilled hot coffee over his legs. Instead of crying, screaming or running for his mother, the little boy solemnly replied to Lady Waldegrave's anxious inquiries: 'Thank you, madam, the agony is abated.'

And even he could not compete with the hopefully apocryphal story of a gentleman standing in a London bus queue whose eye was put out by a careless lady wielding an umbrella. 'It's quite all right, madam,' he is reported to have said, dabbing gently at the blood coursing down his cheek, 'I have another'.

Fighting back

There's no reason why politeness should make you a pushover. For some of us, the Holy Grail of courtesy is the comment that allows us to respond to someone else's rudeness in such a way that we keep our composure, maintain our standards and still manage to squash them as flat as if we'd savaged them with words.

But very few of us manage to do that with the wit, flair and simplicity of Baron Hans Guido von Bülow, the famous German Romantic conductor and composer. Brilliant musician though he was, von Bülow's friends might have been surprised to see him quoted as an example of courtesy, since he had a reputation for tactlessness and plain speaking. Once he is said to have told a trombonist playing in his orchestra, 'Your tone sounds like gravy running through a sewer' – but on this occasion, he reached the heights of cool.

It was the sort of simple incident that happens to everyone; climbing a narrow staircase, he collided with another man coming down. 'Idiot!' the stranger shouted at him angrily.

Von Bülow, in reply, simply raised his hat, extended his hand, and made a slight bow. 'Von Bülow,' he said.

He is the unchallenged champion of the civil but crushing riposte – but an anonymous Italian gentleman from the era of Mussolini might rival him for simple courage. When violently jostled by a stranger on a crowded Rome railway station, he turned to remonstrate angrily with his assailant – to find himself staring at the stout, sweating and swaggering figure of Hermann Göring, Hitler's *Reichsmarschall*, and one of the most powerful men in Nazi Germany.

As the Italian, unperturbed, demanded an apology, Göring thrust out his chest aggressively. 'I am Hermann Göring,' he thundered, expecting him to crumble like everyone else he came into contact with. But the Italian was equal to the bully. 'As an excuse, that is not sufficient,' he replied calmly. 'But as an explanation, it is more than enough.'

Stand aside

The dilemma of a pacifist who is threatened with violence is even more stark than that of a courteous man who has to respond to rudeness. But the mild response of the famous nineteenth-century American Quaker, Joseph Whittall, when he woke to find a burglar in his house, demonstrates that gentle words can mask a steely determination.

'Friend,' he said equably, 'I wish thee would stand to one side. I am about to shoot where thee is standing.'

Do I have your attention?

We have all met those annoying people at parties who carry on a conversation while keeping one eye looking out over your shoulder to see if there is anyone more interesting or influential in the room. One of the first rules of courtesy might be that there is nothing and nobody more important than the person with whom you are speaking.

As Sir Michael Adeane, later Baron Adeane, could have testified.

For twenty years, he was principal private secretary to the queen at Buckingham Palace, where one day he was observed walking calmly but purposefully towards the front of the building. The writer Basil Boothroyd, who was researching his biography of Prince Philip, caught sight of him and hurried to intercept him with a question about the work he was doing.

Sir Michael listened carefully as Boothroyd explained his problem at some length – but after several minutes, the writer began to pick up the merest hint that there was something else fighting for his attention, and politely asked if he was detaining him.

'No, no,' said Sir Michael. 'It's just that … Well, I do hope you'll forgive me, but I've just heard that my house is on fire. It wouldn't matter, but since it is part of St James' Palace …'

Extreme table manners

The controversial Paul Liebrandt, who has spent ten years as one of New York's most original and avant-garde chefs, has perhaps in the past occasionally overstepped the boundaries of good taste. Combinations of eel and chocolate or onions and sorbet were one thing; inviting his guests to lap up foie gras from their soup with their wrists bound was quite another.

Now, established as a serious and highly respected restaurateur, he dismisses such antics as a part of his early search for publicity – but one stunt won't go away. If you read about Liebrandt, you can't miss the story of the guests who were invited to peel jelly from the back of a naked woman, stretched out along the table in a smoke-filled room.

Today, he shrugs it off. 'Half of them didn't even realise it was a real woman until one guy poked her bum,' he told *Esquire* magazine.

And so what does that have to do with a book about manners and courtesy? Just this: in the unlikely event that you are ever invited to eat your dinner off the back of a naked woman, it is considered the mark of a gentleman to be careful with his fork.

And if you are opening a restaurant, you should remember that the craziest publicity stunts will one day come back to haunt you.

A small mistake

There may be some people who are as polite, courteous and charming behind their own front doors as they are in public – but the Scottish judge Lord Braxfield was not one of them. He was evocatively described by his fellow judge, Lord Cockburn, as being 'strong built and dark, with rough eyebrows, powerful eyes, threatening lips, and a low growling voice, he was like a formidable blacksmith', and his manners matched his appearance.

Braxfield, one of the cruellest judges to sit in Scotland in the eighteenth century – a title for which there was considerable competition – was playing a hand of whist one night when he became annoyed by the way his partner was playing.

'What d'ye think ye're doing, ye damned auld bitch!' he growled at her – and then, suddenly collecting his thoughts and squinting across the table, added: 'Your pardon's begged, madam. I took ye for my ain wife.'

It's only fair to the judge to point out that even outside his own family circle, his manners were not particularly gentle. His favourite maxim, uttered whenever prosecutors suggested that there may not be legal grounds for punishing supposed enemies of King George, was 'Let them bring me prisoners, and I'll find 'em law', and he worked long and hard to justify his reputation as the Hanging Judge.

Giving up your seat for a lady

Bringing up children is one of the most challenging of tasks, and teaching them manners may be one of the hardest parts – especially if they sometimes may have reason to doubt your own motives. Take the case of the American writer, poet and humorist Oliver Herford, who was riding on a bus one day with his young nephew.

The bus was crowded, and Herford had the boy on his lap, when an attractive young woman got on. There was no seat for her, so she had to stand. 'Get up, lad, and offer the lady your seat,' Herford urged the boy.

It's not known whether the boy did as he was told – or if he did, what sort of response he received.

A soft answer

Richard Tapper Cadbury, nineteenth-century father of the founder of the famous chocolate manufacturers, was a kindly, gentle and unfailingly courteous man – but instead of aggression, he had a ready wit and a quick tongue.

Walking through Birmingham one day in his homespun Quaker clothes, he came face to face on a narrow pavement with a sumptuously turned out dandy, who looked for a moment with a supercilious smile at the older man's simple dress and humble demeanour. 'I don't step aside for fools,' drawled the dandy.

Cadbury smiled. 'But I do,' he said pointedly – and stepped aside.

A tipping dilemma

Early in the last century, the American writer and academic Rufus Jones was entertaining a rather grand English friend at his home in Haverford, Pennsylvania. Each night, like a true aristocrat, his guest left his shoes outside his bedroom door so that the maid could clean them.

Jones, however, who lived in a simple and unpretentious style, had no servants in his house – and so each night, he quietly took the shoes and polished them himself.

On the morning when he was leaving, his guest put a hand in his pocket. 'Here is a dollar – would you pass it on to the girl who cleans the shoes?' he asked. Jones, unwilling to embarrass his guest, nodded and took the money. 'I'll see that she gets it,' he said.

A sentimental moment

Especially when we are talking to children, courtesy or kindness can sometimes descend almost imperceptibly into sentimentality – which is dangerous, because children can be the most unsentimental of creatures. Take the case of an old friend who had the misfortune to see his 10-year-old daughter injured while she was skiing.

He tried to comfort her as she lay helplessly on the snow, waiting for the paramedics to arrive with the ominously-named 'blood wagon', and then, a little later, followed as they skied down the mountain with her strapped to a stretcher between them. In fact, she had simply twisted her knee – a painful accident, but one that caused no lasting damage – but he didn't know that at the time.

That afternoon, with her leg strapped and bandaged after a lengthy session in the doctor's surgery and with everyone else away on the slopes, they sat and drank large mugs of hot chocolate together in the resort. My friend felt an almost physical pain of his own as he remembered her pale shocked face in the minutes after the collision. 'You know,' he said, 'when I saw you lying in the snow this morning, I would have given anything for it to have been me rather than you that was hurt.'

She looked back at him with big, wide, honest eyes. 'Me too,' she said.

The importance of a smile

Simple, everyday courtesy doesn't have to be complicated – but it's hard to exaggerate how important it can sometimes be. There was a man in his thirties who leapt to his death from San Francisco's Golden Gate Bridge, which enjoys the melancholy accolade of being America's premier location for suicides. Only twenty-eight of the more than 1,300 people who are known to have jumped into the swirling waters of the Pacific nearly 750ft below have survived; remorseless currents carry the bodies of many of the dead out to sea, and they are never found.

This man's body was recovered, however, and the police were able to trace where he had been staying. They went there to see if they could find any information about his background or his identity, and discovered a note he had left behind.

In it, he said that he was going to the bridge to end his life – but that if a single person smiled at him as he was on his way he would turn around and come home. Clearly, nobody did.

A late-night altercation

One of the many stories which the great French playwright Alexandre Dumas, *fils* – son of the famous novelist – most enjoyed hearing told about himself involved his serene handling of a small conjugal difficulty. He had returned unexpectedly from a ball, which he had attended alone, to find his wife, Ida, already in bed. It was winter, and the rest of the house was freezing cold, although there was a roaring fire in her bedroom. So, ignoring Ida's protestations that she wanted to be left alone to sleep, he sat down to read for a little while in front of the fire.

After a few minutes the door to Ida's private bathroom was suddenly flung open with a crash, and Dumas' friend Roger de Beauvoir – a Romantic novelist with a great reputation as a ladies' man – burst into the room, wearing nothing but his shirt. 'This is very embarrassing,' he said, 'but I'm freezing to death in there while you warm yourself by the fire.'

Men had fought duels with less provocation, and Dumas was understandably shocked and furious. There was an angry exchange, at the end of which he began to manhandle the interloper out of his house. When he opened the door to an icy blast of wind, however, and saw the rain pelting down, he paused; de Beauvoir was an old friend, after all, it was a bitter night and in any case, he and his wife were not particularly close. They did, after all, have separate bedrooms. More to the point, perhaps, Dumas had a certain reputation of his own. It could, he reasoned, have been him hiding in the darkness in a strange bathroom.

He shut the door again, and ushered de Beauvoir back into the room. 'We'll discuss this tomorrow,' he said. 'For the time being, you take my chair by the fire, and I'll get into bed.'

But as the fire died down and de Beauvoir huddled closer and closer to the embers, the noise of his chattering teeth and shivering woke Dumas again. 'Oh, come to bed,' he shouted, and de Beauvoir slipped between the sheets on the other side of Ida – and so they stayed, with Dumas' wife either sleeping or pretending to sleep soundly with her husband on one side and her lover on the other.

Dumas was the first to wake, and leaning over his wife, he shook de Beauvoir by the shoulder. 'I've been thinking,' he said. 'Why should old friends break up over a woman, even a wife?'

Perhaps, for modern tastes, this was taking courtesy a little far, and maybe Ida's opinion might have been canvassed. But Dumas certainly had style.

The odd couple

Marriage can be entered into for all sorts of reasons: love, lust, social ambition or simple financial greed. Sometimes, as in the case of Erika Mann and W.H. Auden, it can be a matter of kindness and generosity, mixed with the need to outwit a tyrannical government.

In 1935 the 30-year-old Mann, a popular actress and writer, was threatened with the loss of her German citizenship in retaliation for her role in devising *The Pepper Mill*, a satirical cabaret review which ridiculed the Nazi regime. She was gay, and she appealed to her friend and fellow-homosexual, the novelist Christopher Isherwood, to marry her so that she could obtain an English passport.

Isherwood was unwilling to help, but he described her plight to Auden, who immediately agreed to become her husband. Since he was also homosexual, the marriage between the two partners – who had not even met until a few days before the ceremony – was a complete sham, but it enabled Mann to escape from Nazi Germany and the two became good friends when they were living in New York.

Erika went on to make arrangements for scores of other artists, political dissidents and enemies of the Nazis to escape, and on one occasion approached Auden again. Could he find another homosexual man to help another actress, like herself, who was under threat and needed a foreign passport because of her anti-Nazi activities? Auden found a friend who cheerfully obliged, and another anti-Nazi activist was saved from probable imprisonment and death.

Auden himself affected not to understand why Erika was so grateful. 'After all, what are buggers for?' he asked cheerfully.

Marks of mutual respect

The controversial Tory politician Enoch Powell could be impatient, even irascible, but in his personal relationships, he was punctilious about good manners. In the 1980s, the Irish-born Conservative journalist, writer and political polemicist Patrick Cosgrave (1941–2001) was commissioned to write his official biography, for which Powell granted him access to his files of correspondence. This entailed Cosgrave visiting Powell at his house in London, where a room had been set aside for him to work in. There he found all the paraphernalia a writer might need: desk and chair, paper and writing implements, files of documents he might want to consult, plus he also had access to Powell himself.

Both were courteous men, but Powell passionately disliked smoking, whereas Patrick smoked heavily. On the desk each day, Cosgrave would find a clean ashtray. On the desk each evening, when the writer left, Powell would also find a clean and unused ashtray. Each man, consistently, silently and generously, deferred to the wishes of the other. This is, it's true, only a small story, but it speaks much for their mutual respect.

The kindness of strangers

Dom Joly was the star of the wildly successful *Trigger Happy TV*, a hidden-camera comedy series that ran on British TV for two series in 2000 and 2001. In October 2008, in one of his weekly columns in *The Independent on Sunday*, the British television comedian and journalist Joly told of the kindness of a stranger in Los Angeles as the world's financial crisis continued to deepen.

He was filming a sketch in the middle of the banking district of the city, playing the part of a desperate and bedraggled financial trader. He stood in the street, apparently lost. His business suit was dishevelled, his briefcase was hanging wide open and empty, and there was a panic-stricken look in his eyes. He was clearly a victim of the credit crunch. Nervous bankers crossed the street to avoid him and turned their faces away, as if by speaking to him, touching him or even passing close by him they might somehow be infected by his bad luck. But then, suddenly, one of them broke ranks and came over to him.

'Hey buddy, you OK?' he asked with a look of deep concern. Joly was too embarrassed to admit that he was acting a part; the Good Samaritan had clearly not noticed the film camera with the huge zoom lens on the other side of the street, and Joly was not going to point it out to him.

'I ... lost my job today, they just came and said it was all over ... I've got nothing.'

Joly was throwing his heart and soul into the performance. His new friend smiled softly.

'Don't worry, buddy, the whole country is going through a tough time right now but we'll get through it. We've just got to stand together. I lost my job two years back but I got it together and so will you. What sector are you in, do you want some lunch? Maybe I can help you?'

Joly was staggered – it was an extraordinary gesture of random and completely unexpected generosity. Banking crisis or no banking crisis, Joly concluded, all is definitely not lost in the USA.

4

THE GREAT &
THE GOOD

By and large, diplomats, politicians, government ministers and other pillars of society don't get a very good press. All too often their jobs involve protecting their dignity, and it is easy for them to seem pompous and self-important. But when they are not dealing with great matters of public policy or kept at a distance by officials or press secretaries, they feel ordinary emotions and they speak to ordinary people.

Beneath their crowns, chains of office or diplomatic honours, they have the same faults and virtues as everybody else, and a flash of humour, a moment's generosity or even an ironic raised eyebrow can sometimes reveal a real person who may be much more human than anyone ever guessed.

Throughout history, those who have held high office may often have had an inflated idea of their own importance; they may have seemed stiff and unapproachable, and their motives may sometimes have been questionable. But when their ordinary human kindness does show through, it's hard to doubt the sincerity of courtesy which is extended to those from whom they need neither fear injury nor hope for gain from.

Your obedient enemy

Sometimes, extravagant courtesy can be used to make a point, as in the case of Winston Churchill and his punctilious little note of December 1941 to the Japanese ambassador, declaring war. No doubt it was partly the result of having 'the right way to behave' drummed into him as a child – but the story, told in the Commons, also enabled him to score several very public points for cool and confidence. The note read as follows:

Sir,

On the evening of December 7th His Majesty's Government in the United Kingdom learned that Japanese forces without previous warning either in the form of a declaration of war or of an ultimatum with a conditional declaration of war had attempted a landing on the coast of Malaya and bombed Singapore and Hong Kong.

In view of these wanton acts of unprovoked aggression committed in flagrant violation of International Law and particularly of Article I of the Third Hague Convention relative to the opening of hostilities, to which both Japan and the United Kingdom are parties, His Majesty's Ambassador at Tokyo has been instructed to inform the Imperial Japanese Government in the name of His Majesty's Government in the United Kingdom that a state of war exists between our two countries.

> I have the honour to be, with high consideration, Sir,
> Your obedient servant,
> Winston S. Churchill

Churchill was criticised for his extravagantly respectful words. However, he later wrote of it, 'Some people did not like this ceremonial style. But after all, when you have to kill a man, it costs nothing to be polite'.

A most superior person

Occasionally, demonstrations of courtesy are so extreme that the suspicion arises that they may not be entirely sincerely meant. Even the most exalted figures in public life may not be above sarcasm. Take the case of the Earl of Derby and the Honourable George Nathaniel, First Marquess Curzon of Kedleston.

The marquess was every bit as grand as his name suggests. As a young student at Oxford in the 1870s, he was lampooned by his contemporaries in the famous rhyme:

My name is George Nathaniel Curzon,
I am a most superior person.

Perhaps the impression of stiffness and pomposity were partly the result of his having to wear a rigid corset because of a spinal injury – or perhaps he was simply an unmitigated and self-important snob. In any case, his appointment as Viceroy to India at the age of 39, and then as Foreign Secretary, did nothing to make him more humble. He delighted in laying down the law to other mortals on all manner of subjects; 'Gentlemen never wear brown in town' was one of his pronouncements. As was his famous advice to his new wife about making love: 'The lady never moves.'

When he was Foreign Secretary even the Prime Minister, David Lloyd George, and his Cabinet colleagues got the full Curzon treatment. He suffered from phlebitis, and would sit grandly in Cabinet meetings with his leg resting on a green baize footstool. Several times, ministers were kept waiting for him with no message, no apology and no explanation.

Eventually, it was too much for the Earl of Derby, Lloyd George's Secretary for War, who was every bit as self-important as Curzon but with a rather more well-developed sense of humour. When a servant arrived, gravely carrying the famous green footstool, and placed it before the Foreign Secretary's empty chair, the noble earl rose to his feet. Bowing solemnly to the footstool, he declared: 'The Marquess himself has not arrived, but we see premonitory symptoms'.

A matter of honour

In modern politics, no quarter is asked for or given. If a minister's carelessness or indiscretion hands the opposition a stick with which to beat him, he can confidently expect a sound and public thrashing, either in parliament, in the newspapers or on television. It was not always so.

Sir Robert Peel and Benjamin Disraeli, two giants of the Conservative Party in nineteenth-century politics, loathed each other. In Disraeli's case, this dislike went back to a perceived slight when he had written a private letter to Peel in an unsuccessful plea for a place in his government. His wife added her own personal appeal, with the rider, 'Be pleased not to answer this, as I do not wish any human being to know I have written to you this humble petition'.

The letters were indeed unanswered, and Disraeli received no promotion. This rebuff rankled for several years, and he frequently turned his lacerating wit on the Conservative prime minister. Four years later, provoked beyond endurance, Peel snapped back during a House of Commons debate that Disraeli's criticism came ill from a man who had once been 'ready, as I think he was, to unite his fortunes with mine in office'.

Inexplicably, Disraeli replied with a flat lie. 'I can say that I have never asked a favour of the Government ... With respect to my being a solicitor for office, it is entirely unfounded,' he said. He must have known of the existence of the two letters that would prove he was lying; even as he spoke, he must have realised that he was handing Peel a weapon with which the prime minister could destroy him.

And Peel said – nothing. He merely repeated his original comment, without mentioning the existence of the letters. A political victory was one thing, but reading out personal and private correspondence in public would have been dishonourable and beneath him. It was a matter not just of courtesy to an undeserving political opponent, but of personal honour. Only after more than fifty years, when both men were dead, were the letters finally made public.

Popping the question

There are disadvantages to high position. The dignity of one's office may create a distance from other people that may not always be welcome – and if this is true today, it was even more so in Queen Victoria's time. The trick, even for a young and inexperienced woman and even for a monarch as concerned with propriety as Victoria, was to sweep away the conventions when they threatened to get in the way.

In December 1830, the 21-year-old queen was about to inform the Privy Council of her decision to marry Prince Albert of Saxe-Coburg and Gotha. One of the ladies of her court, the Duchess of Gloucester, asked her whether such a solemn announcement did not make her feel nervous.

'Not at all,' the queen replied. 'But it was a nervous thing to propose to Prince Albert.'

'What! Did *you* propose to *him*?' asked the duchess, as shocked as it is permissible to be with one's sovereign.

'To be sure I did,' said the queen. 'He would never have taken such a liberty as to propose to the Queen of England.'

This momentous act of courtesy by the young queen to her future husband – who was himself only 20 years old at the time – led to a marriage that produced nine children, and which remained close and passionate until his death at the early age of 42.

Things were done much better

Queen Alexandra, the consort of King Edward VII, behaved with impeccable dignity throughout her married life, as scandal after scandal about her husband's affairs with actresses, singers, court ladies and members of London's demi-monde were whispered about and hushed up.

As the king lay dying, she welcomed his last mistress, Alice Keppel, to the little group at his death bed. Great-great-grandmother of the present Duchess of Cornwall, Keppel was a well-known courtesan with a list of past lovers that looked like a page from Debrett's. The king was the latest of a long line of aristocratic lovers to share her favours.

But Queen Alexandra, who was well aware of her liaison with Edward, shook her by the hand. 'I am sure you always had a good influence on him,' she said gently.

Alice Keppel, incidentally, was clearly appreciative of Alexandra's forbearance and courtesy. Nearly three decades later, whilst dining at the Ritz, the 70-year-old *grande horizontale* was told that her lover's grandson, King Edward VIII, was abdicating the throne to marry his lover, Wallis Simpson. 'Things were done much better in my day,' she observed.

Being nice to Hitler

In today's era of cocksure television presenters, it may be hard to think of the BBC as the sober-sided mouthpiece of the nation, desperate to avoid causing offence. Back in the thirties, though, these things mattered – sometimes, perhaps, a little too much.

The comedian Ronald Frankau, descended from a German Jewish family, submitted a song which he planned to sing in a BBC broadcast, containing the words 'Let's find Hitler and kick him in the pants'. BBC executives decided, after consulting the Foreign Office, that it might be found offensive by the German Chancellor.

Might it be possible to drop Hitler's name, and substitute 'Carnera' – the name of an Italian heavyweight boxer – they suggested, apparently not noticing that the new line would not scan, would not be funny and would not make sense. Men who sit in offices seldom have a sense of humour.

Frankau certainly did not find their suggestion funny, and the song was never performed – but the BBC retained its reputation for politeness and courtesy, and no offence was caused to Adolf Hitler or the Nazis.

Bearing a grudge

In their official capacity, members of the Royal Family always try to avoid disputes. It would be discourteous in the extreme, for instance, to tell a guest at a royal function that he is talking rubbish – far better to say something bland and avoid controversy.

However, they don't need actually to agree. So maybe the late Queen Mother went a little far when she was introduced to a leathery-skinned old Boer farmer from South Africa at a garden party.

'I can never forgive the English for the way they raped and occupied my country,' he said – still unsmiling, some eighty years after the end of the Boer War.

The Queen Mother smiled indulgently. 'I quite understand,' she replied conspiratorially. 'We feel much the same in Scotland.'

Lost in translation

Occasionally, just occasionally, it may be necessary to sacrifice truth in order to preserve courtesy. Her Highness Princess Charlotte Sophia of Mecklenburg-Strelitz, who travelled to London in 1761 to marry the young King George III, was not, to put it kindly, conventionally pretty. She had a wide, flat face, big ears, a large mouth and a snub pug nose – in fact, although King George's courtiers would have been much too polite to suggest it, it was generally agreed that she looked like a dog.

The crowds who thronged the streets to see her coach pass by, however, did not share the reticence of the court. 'Pug!' they shouted. 'Pug!'

The princess, whose grasp of English was as limited as her beauty, turned to her lady-in-waiting, the Duchess of Ancaster. 'Vat is this vord they are saying? Vat means *poog*?'

Without a pause, the duchess replied, tactfully but maybe not entirely convincingly: 'It means "God bless Your Royal Highness."'

The story, like the London crowd, is less than fair to the princess, who was not only a keen and dedicated amateur botanist, but also a noted patron of the arts. She was also a loyal consort to King George and bore him fifteen children, remaining at his side throughout the illness which left him, in the poet Shelley's cruel words, 'an old, mad, blind, despised and dying king'.

A gentle reminder

A young European diplomat was invited to dinner with Grover Cleveland, twenty-second and twenty-fourth President of the United States, and his wife Frances Folsom Cleveland during Cleveland's second term of office in the 1890s. Cleveland was the only president ever to be voted out of office and then return to the White House for a second term – and also the only president to be married while in office. His wife, who was renowned for her beauty and good humour, and who became one of the most popular first ladies ever to live in the White House, was only 21 when they married in 1886 during his first term, but she developed a clear eye for social etiquette.

Their young dinner guest was about to tuck into the salad with which he had been served when he noticed a large and particularly unpleasant-looking worm lurking under a leaf. He was about to call one of the staff to point this out when he caught Mrs Cleveland's eye, observing him narrowly. Nothing was said, not even an eyebrow was raised, but her meaning was clear; any complaint would not go down well with the president.

The diplomat meekly ate his salad, worm and all. The First Lady nodded and smiled. 'Young man, you will go a long way,' she said. Fifteen years later he returned to Washington, not as a junior diplomat, but as his country's ambassador.

Punctuality & the politeness of kings

King George V always insisted on strict punctuality, particularly at mealtimes – the royal family were expected to sit down together each evening for a formal dinner. Nothing annoyed the king more than lateness at the table.

At the same time, however, King George was very fond of his new daughter-in-law, the former Elizabeth Bowes-Lyon. She was later to be King George VI's Queen Elizabeth, and subsequently the universally respected Queen Mother – but on this occasion, only in her twenties and the new wife of the king's second son, she committed the cardinal sin of arriving late in the royal dining room.

She apologised profusely and waited nervously as everyone anticipated an explosion of wrath from the notoriously short-tempered king. Instead he smiled indulgently, ostentatiously consulted his pocket watch, and said: 'You are not late, my dear. I think we must have sat down two minutes early.'

Don't stand on ceremony

The mark of a true gentleman is that he inspires respect without ever seeming to try to do so. Henry Kissinger,

American Secretary of State under President Richard Nixon, however, could be a stickler for etiquette. At an official reception, impatient with the nervous dithering of a young guest, he growled, 'I never stand on protocol. Just call me Your Excellency.'

Much the same thing happened to the future Poet Laureate, John Betjeman, as a young man when he became engaged to his future wife Penelope Chetwode. Her parents did not approve of the match, but her father, Field Marshall Lord Chetwode of the Indian army, made what he clearly thought was a generous conciliatory gesture. 'Well Betjeman,' he barked to the nervous suitor, 'if you're going to be my son-in-law, you needn't go on calling me "Sir". Just call me "Field Marshal".'

Follow that car

The American politician and diplomat Averell Harriman held high office under several American presidents, and was ambassador to the Soviet Union in the final years of the Second World War, before coming to London as ambassador in 1946. Although the Americans and the Russians were allies in the fight against Hitler, the KGB had orders from Stalin that Harriman was to be kept under close surveillance.

No one bothered to try to hide the fact that he was followed everywhere he went by the secret police. One winter weekend, he set off to visit a British diplomat at his country home outside Moscow, considerately warning the two agents shadowing him that they would need a four-wheel-drive vehicle to negotiate the rough country roads.

The Russians, presumably thinking that they needed no advice from a foreigner about how to cope with the winter weather, ignored his advice and set off after him in their heated but quite unsuitable saloon car. Before long it got bogged down in the mud and snow, as Harriman had warned, so he ordered his driver to slow down so that one of the secret policemen, following on foot, could keep up.

Slowly the official car made its way up the road until Harriman, worried that the Russian might freeze to death and presumably wanting to speed up his own journey, stopped and offered him a ride, promising not to tell anyone about it. The KGB was not known for its sense of humour, and the agent might have faced savage punishment, but the man accepted, and the ambassador and his secret police 'tail' finished the journey sitting side by side in the American Embassy's car. Harriman kept his promise until his memoirs were published some thirty years later.

In fact, the KGB may well have learned about it some time earlier through their own nefarious channels. In 1945 Harriman was presented with a wooden carving of the Great Seal of the United States, which was duly given pride of place in Spaso House – then, as now, the official Moscow residence of the American ambassador. Seven years later, it was found to have been bugged so that the Soviet secret service could eavesdrop on the ambassador's private conversations.

An ambiguous gesture

Thomas Jefferson, the third President of the United States, was a convinced and dedicated abolitionist – but also a lifelong slave-owner. It was a contradiction that he struggled with all his life, and one that biographers still argue about. It is accepted that by the standards of his time, he treated his slaves well, having many of them educated and others trained in practical skills. But he still believed that blacks were by nature inferior to their white masters.

One frequently repeated story describes how he was out in a carriage one day with his grandson near his mountain-top estate of Monticello in Virginia. A slave who was walking in the road, and whom neither Jefferson nor his grandson knew, politely doffed his hat to them. Jefferson, as he always did, took off his own hat and acknowledged the gesture, but his grandson simply kept talking, ignoring the man.

Jefferson turned to him, frowning. 'Do you permit a slave to be more of a gentleman than you are?' he asked severely.

It's possible, reflecting Jefferson's own ambiguity, to see that exchange either as the behaviour of a racist who assumed that his own white family should be superior in every way to the black slaves that they owned, or as that of a man of impeccable courtesy insisting that everyone should be treated with respect. Either way, it was another thirty-five years before the end of America's bloody Civil War settled the question of slavery forever.

The assassin who couldn't shoot

Frenchmen, as everybody knows, are passionate and excitable – or at least that is the stereotype. There is, people occasionally joke, no word in French for sangfroid. But Georges Clemenceau, Prime Minister of France at the end of the First World War, believed that calm composure was first cousin to courtesy.

As preparations were being made for the Treaty of Versailles, which would formally end the war, Clemenceau was fired on in an assassination attempt by a young anarchist, Emile Cottin. Cottin loosed off seven shots from a revolver, grazing the elderly statesman's head with one bullet.

The crowd nearly lynched Cottin, but Clemenceau remarked calmly:

> We have just won the most terrible war in history, yet here is a Frenchman who misses his target six times out of seven. Of course the fellow must be punished for the careless use of a dangerous weapon. Eight years in prison with intensive training in a shooting gallery.

In fact, Cottin was sentenced to death, but later had his sentence commuted to ten years in prison. It is not known whether he managed to improve his shooting. He later died while fighting in the Spanish Civil War.

Free & easy

Whatever else diplomats manage when abroad in a foreign country, they can usually be relied on to get the protocol right – and when they try to bend the rules a little, they can come sadly unstuck.

The journalist Frank Giles, one-time editor of *The Sunday Times*, was travelling abroad with his wife when they were invited to a formal Embassy dinner – some versions of this story say it was the American Embassy, others, the British. The invitation was addressed to Mr and Mrs Frank Giles – which, as Giles' wife Katherine was the daughter of an earl and retained her title, was something of a breach of protocol. She should have been addressed as Lady Katherine Giles.

So Giles rang the Embassy to point out the error. He wasn't complaining, he started gently, but the lady accompanying him wasn't exactly *Mrs* Giles. The member of the Embassy staff at the other end of the phone cut him off in mid-sentence.

'That's OK, don't worry about it,' he said encouragingly. 'Bring her along anyway. We're not a bit stuffy here.'

A gentleman?

John Dalrymple, second Earl of Stair and King George I's ambassador to Paris, was a man with a reputation. He was, the elderly Earl of Chesterfield declared approvingly, the most 'finished' gentleman he ever knew.

This 'finish' – breeding or good taste, in modern terms – held him in good stead. He was a favourite of King Louis XIV, who decided to put his reputedly exquisite manners to an idiosyncratic test. As they got into a carriage together, the king stood aside to allow him to mount the steps first. Without a pause, the earl climbed into the carriage before him. On the face of it, a shocking breach of etiquette, but one that seemed to please the king.

'It is true what I have heard, for this man did not trouble me with ceremony, whereas one less polite, would have stood bowing, and making a thousand excuses and apologies for refusing what I desired,' he said.

On another occasion, the earl was at a dinner where his fellow diplomats were vying with each other in extravagant praise of their monarchs. The French ambassador, the Abbé de Ville, proposed a toast to 'the Rising Sun', by which he meant King Louis. The Austrian ambassador, the Baron de Reisbach, replied with a toast to 'the Moon', referring to the empress. Then it was the Earl of Stair's turn and he, referring to a Biblical verse, proposed a toast to the King of England as 'Joshua, who made the sun and moon stand still'. It was a quip that can have done him no harm at all when repeated back at court in London.

So the earl had the invaluable gifts for a diplomat of wit and charm. But there was, too, a side to his character that may have been less savoury.

He had an enviable reputation for pleasing the ladies of King Louis' court, and playing cards one night, he lent a thousand *louis d'or* to the Duchess of Maine, a relative of the French king and a woman of immense influence who had suffered a run of bad luck. Summoned to see her next day, he brushed aside her pleas that he should say nothing about the loan, which would have been extremely embarrassing to her.

'I had already forgotten it myself, and should never have recollected it again had not Your Highness put my memory to the rack by refreshing it,' he smiled. A characteristically generous and chivalrous gesture, on the face of it – except that soon afterwards, the duchess began passing him important and confidential information. Was it a coincidence, or had she been blackmailed? Or bribed? Either way, it's not an incident that reflects particularly well on the exquisite Earl of Stair.

An aristocrat, perhaps, but not entirely a gentleman.

Grace under pressure

History has not been kind to Marie Antoinette, the queen of Louis XVI of France, who died on the guillotine in the French Revolution. Everybody recalls how when told that the people of Paris were starving and could get no bread, she said '*Qu'ils mangent de la brioche!*' ('Let them eat cake!') – which may or may not be true.

No one has said where or when she made the remark, which sounds like a piece of post-Revolutionary propaganda. It certainly wasn't an original comment –

indeed it was quoted as a current saying at least fifty years before her time.

But in any case, there are other, more believable, stories that show the young French queen in a much more sensitive and courteous light. Probably the most poignant describes her on the scaffold, about to be executed in front of the baying mob.

Stepping towards the guillotine, she accidentally trod on the executioner's foot. Pale and trembling, she turned and bowed slightly towards the man who was about to cut off her head. 'I ask your pardon, Monsieur,' she said. 'I did not do it on purpose.'

The 'Merry Monarch' & the queen who was not amused

William Penn, the founder of the American state of Pennsylvania, was a Quaker and believed passionately in the equality of all men before God – a belief that was commonly put into practice among his fellow Quakers by a refusal to remove their hats when introduced to people.

This minor social embarrassment could have been a serious breach of etiquette when he found himself in the presence of King Charles II – but luckily, the king had a sense of humour. It was not for nothing that he was known as the 'Merry Monarch'. With a flourish and a bow he removed his own hat.

'Friend Charles,' said Penn – the unusual form of address another mark of his Quaker beliefs – 'Why dost thou take off thy hat?'

'Friend Penn,' the king replied, with a smile. 'Dost thou not know that in this place it is the custom that only one man at a time should keep his hat on?'

Queen Victoria, however, was famous for being less easily amused, as the Irish peer Michael William de Courcy, 32nd Baron Kingsale – and thus heir to one of the oldest titles in Britain or Ireland – discovered. He appeared at court and attempted to take advantage of a privilege that had allegedly been granted to his forebears by King John some 600 years earlier: allowing them to appear before the monarch without removing their hats. (Some authorities suggest that if this privilege was ever granted at all, it may well have been because the noble lord's hair was infested with lice.)

The queen looked at him for a moment, nonplussed. Then, when the baron explained the ancient legend, she scoffed. 'Don't be so silly,' she said briskly. 'You may have the right to keep your hat on before your monarch, but I happen to be a lady as well. Take it off at once!'

Confrontation with the emperor

There is no shortage of anecdotes about the great and powerful behaving well. Those, after all, are the one they would like to see repeated. For sheer vulgarity, met with aristocratic good breeding, it is hard to beat the story of Napoleon's confrontation with his Grand Chamberlain, Charles-Maurice de Talleyrand-Périgord.

Talleyrand was a subtle, scheming and serpentine French diplomat and statesman, who had already served under Louis XVI through the French Revolution, and would go on to hold office under Louis XVIII, Charles X and Louis Philippe as well.

There is confusion over what sparked Napoleon's wrath; some accounts say that it was Talleyrand's opposition to his invasion of Spain and Portugal, others that the emperor suspected him of plotting his assassination. What is known, however, is that Napoleon summoned a meeting of his council on 28 January 1809, at which he turned on Talleyrand in the most abusive way.

In front of all the other ministers, he raged and swore at him, finally screaming in his face: '*Tenez, vous êtes de la merde dans un bas do soie!*' ('You're a piece of shit in a silk stocking!') – a forceful but unconventional description. There was a moment's silence as the aristocratic and refined Talleyrand stared at the emperor. Then, as Napoleon stormed out of the room, he murmured disdainfully, 'What a pity that such a great man should be so ill bred!'

That barely disguised contempt, however, did not prevent Talleyrand from continuing to serve Napoleon assiduously – at least until it became clear that the French monarchy was likely to return, at which point he reconciled himself with the surviving exiled members of the Bourbon dynasty. After all, another of his famous sayings was 'Regimes may fall and fail, but I do not'.

An expression of trust

Throughout history, and often with good cause, kings, generals and great leaders have lived their lives in a fog of suspicion, unable to trust even their closest servants. They have been surrounded by guards, with food tasters constantly on call to protect them against the risk of poison. The courts of the mighty were seldom a healthy place to live.

The Greek chronicler Plutarch tells a story about Alexander the Great that demonstrates the atmosphere of fear and distrust that encompassed his followers – and the nobility with which he responded to it.

Marching through Asia Minor on the way to his great victories over the Persians, the emperor fell dangerously ill, possibly as a result of swimming in the icy waters of the River Cydnus. His most respected physicians did not dare to treat him, since they realised that if they failed and Alexander died, they would be accused of having killed him. Only one doctor, Philip the Arcanian, had both the confidence and the courage to attend the ailing emperor. It would be, Philip thought, the highest ingratitude not to try to save his life through fear for his own, and so he brought his drugs and medicines into Alexander's tent.

However, Alexander had received a letter warning him to beware of Philip who, the letter-writer said, had been bribed by the Persian King Darius to poison him. He read it and hid it under his pillow without telling anyone, before summoning Philip to bring his medicine. Alexander took the cup, and as he drank it, he handed Philip the letter.

Philip was both outraged and terrified by the accusation, and threw himself on the ground by Alexander's bed, begging the emperor to trust him – and the response from the sick leader was that he had complete faith in Philip's honour and in his medical skill. The medicine was so powerful that it left Alexander in a coma for a while – which must have been a tense time for Philip – but after three days he was well enough to lead his army again.

A poor harvest

The summer of 1783 in France was cold and wet, and the harvest was correspondingly poor, but because the estates of the wealthy Marquis de Lafayette were so extensive, his barns were still well-filled with wheat. The head bailiff pointed out that with prices at record levels because of the shortages, it would be a good time to sell.

But Lafayette – later to play an important role in the American Revolution and become the firm friend of George Washington – had seen the hungry families in the villages of the Auvergne. 'No, this is a good time to give,' he said.

5

A WORLD ELSEWHERE

The English may sometimes like to pretend that good manners were their gift to the world, but other peoples and other cultures have a very different view. Certainly George Bernard Shaw – an Irishman who enjoyed teasing the English – thought that English courtesy left a lot to be desired.

'We don't bother much about dress and manners in England, because, as a rule, we don't dress well and we've no manners,' says a character in one of his plays.

In fact, the famous British self-confidence and insouciance may come across as something quite different to people in other countries. The contrast between the Americans and the British when travelling abroad, according to one assessment, is that Americans behave as if they own the country, while the British behave as if they don't care who owns the country.

The truth is that every culture has its own idea of the proper way to behave. Sometimes, offence may be taken where none was intended. A businessman whose manner would seem laudably brisk and efficient in London or New York would simply seem brash and vulgar in the Arab world; eating with your fingers at a state banquet in Buckingham Palace would cause outrage, but in Beijing, no one would raise an eyebrow. Diplomatic parties in Thailand sometimes resemble slow waltzes around the room, as western guests stand up close to their Thai hosts to speak to them, leading the Thais to back away gently to preserve their personal space.

These, though, are the details of behaviour. Courtesy – putting oneself imaginatively in someone else's place, behaving with consideration, showing hospitality – is valued everywhere.

A generous man

Wilfred Thesiger, the great Arabian traveller of the twentieth century, was not sentimental about the Arabs. In *Arabian Sands*, his classic account of the crossing of the Empty Quarter, he describes with horror the murder of a young child in a tribal blood feud, and hears an account of a gruesome public execution in Riyadh.

But he had no doubt about the generosity, hospitality and courtesy of the bedu tribesmen with whom he travelled. 'The only society in which I have found nobility is that of the bedu,' he said in an interview, years after his wanderings were over.

Again and again, he describes his generous welcome at the hands of strangers – shopkeepers who greet him, sit with him, send for tea and forget to try to sell him anything; or complete strangers who invite him to lunch or dinner. 'I have wondered sadly what Arabs brought up in this tradition have thought when they visited England; and I have hoped that they realised that we are as unfriendly to each other as we must appear to be to them,' he says.

On one occasion an old man in a torn and scruffy loincloth, clearly a beggar, joined Thesiger and his companions at their camp in the desert. Thesiger – a generous enough man by his own rights – gave him a few coins, but was astonished by the warmth of the welcome offered to the old man by the bedu tribesmen.

They explained quietly to him that the guest was not just a poverty-stricken old man, but a famous member of the Bait Imani tribe, widely respected for his generosity. But how could such a man be so generous, Thesiger wondered, looking at the threadbare clothes, the broken sheath of his old dagger and the sagging skin on the starving body. 'I should not have thought he owned anything to be generous with.'

That's true, the Arab explained: once, their guest had been one of the richest men in the tribe, but now all he owned was a few scrawny goats – not a camel, not a wife, not even a son, since his child had been killed a couple of years before by raiders. 'What happened to his camels?' Thesiger asked, still not understanding. 'Did raiders taken them, or did they die of disease?'

No, nothing like that, came the patient reply. He had given everything away, killing his camels to feed strangers who came to his tent; he was ruined by his own generosity. 'By God, he is generous!' the bedu tribesman said, and Thesiger, understanding at last, could hear the envy in his voice.

The blind eye of a gentleman

The Arabs still value the idea of generosity. A western girl, some years ago, was hurrying to her job as a newsreader at Qatar Television, in the Gulf, when she had to stop for petrol. After paying for her fuel, she reversed her heavy four-wheel-drive so that she could leave the petrol station in such haste that she failed to notice the large and shiny Mercedes that had pulled in behind her.

Crash! Her car, with its big no-nonsense bumpers, was unmarked, but the front of the Mercedes was a mangled mess of bent chrome and dented paintwork.

Flustered and embarrassed, she got out to apologise to the driver, an elderly white-robed Arab. 'I'm terribly sorry, the accident was entirely my fault,' she said – slightly unnecessarily, since his car had been stationary when she had hit it. 'I'm afraid I can't stop because I'm late for work, but these are my details.'

Ignoring her proffered card, he looked at the mangled remains of the front of his car. 'Accident?' he said. 'What accident? You should get on your way into work.'

All right, she was young and pretty, and he was clearly rich enough to be able to afford gestures like that. But it was still an act of kindness and courtesy that she remembered for a very long time.

Homeward bound

Thomas Nuttall was a pioneering botanist and zoologist who left his native England early in the nineteenth century to study the flora and fauna of the remote areas of north-west America. His reputation as a scientist was exemplary – he brought back many specimens that were previously unknown to science, and wrote several classic studies of his discoveries – but his standing as an explorer is less sure.

Nuttall suffered from the considerable disadvantage of being unable to find his way. On one plant-hunting expedition he found himself hopelessly lost, and then, terrified by the stories he had heard of savage tribes living in the area, he ran away from the search party which had been sent to find him. He evaded them for three days, until – quite by chance – he stumbled back into camp, with his would-be rescuers hard on his heels.

His fears of attack by the Native Americans were probably justified – the tribes were extremely hostile to incursions into their area. However, when he lost his way in the forest again, he owed his life to the tribesman who found him.

The Native American hunter stumbled upon Nuttall when he had already been lost for hours, and was exhausted and almost unconscious. The great explorer looked so helpless that, rather than scalping the white man and stealing his equipment, he carried him 3 miles to the river, placed him gently in a canoe, and – no doubt wondering how a man who got lost so easily had found his way this far – paddled him back to rejoin the other members of the scientific expedition at their camp.

Unfortunately, the name of this selfless and compassionate rescuer is not recorded. It would be nice to think that, if he ever needed help from the explorers who were trekking through his country, he might have had similar treatment.

The warmest of welcomes

Courtesy and hospitality towards strangers in different times and different places may take forms that would seem bizarre to a twenty-first-century European – but there is no reason to suppose that they were not genuinely meant, and very little doubt that they were extremely well received. Take the story of the Tibetans, told by Marco Polo some 700 years ago.

Tibetan men, he says, prefer to marry women of wide and varied sexual experience – and so when foreigners pass through their country, mothers from miles around hurry to their camp, bringing with them their young and nubile daughters. In a ceremony which sounds rather like some fantasy dreamed up by the editor of a top-shelf lads' magazine, the travellers simply choose the ones they find most attractive, and send the others home disappointed.

The girls then stay with them for as long as they remain in camp; the only rule is that they cannot be taken away. After the travellers have 'worked their will', as Marco Polo delicately puts it, they move on, each one leaving his chosen *inamorata* to return to her village with some small token or trinket to hang around her neck.

To have any chance of catching a suitable husband, the young girls have to build up a collection of twenty or more of these tokens – this gets more and more like the lads' magazine – so there is considerable competition among the girls to gain a place in camp. The girls – at least as far as Marco Polo can see – are happy; the Tibetan men are presumably well pleased with what their future wives have learned. And as for the travellers – well, says Marco Polo, slightly unnecessarily, 'Obviously the country is a fine one to visit for a lad from sixteen to twenty-four.'

Clash of cultures

The one-time Soviet leader Nikita Khrushchev was fond of reminding foreign dignitaries of the many and various cultures that existed under the Soviet umbrella – and particularly of the Cossack tradition of hospitality in the Caucasus. A guest in your home, sharing your bread and salt, should be treated with the greatest hospitality, even if he is your bitter enemy, he used to say. 'But once he steps outside your door, then you can slit his throat.'

Many of the Cossacks had, of course, opposed the Communist revolution from the beginning; many had fought alongside the Nazis against Soviet troops in the Second World War. So maybe Khrushchev was biased against them. In any case, it hardly lay in his mouth to offer lectures on civility – he was known for his rough temper and furious rages.

During debates at the United Nations General Assembly in 1960, when the atmosphere was tense after the shooting down of an American U2 spy plane over Russia, he repeatedly interrupted proceedings by thumping on the desk with his fist and shouting angrily at the speakers.

When a delegate from the Philippines accused the Soviets of imperialism in Eastern Europe, Khrushchev famously took off his shoe and hammered it repeatedly on the desk, almost drowning out the delegate's speech. In response, Britain's urbane and aristocratic Prime Minister Harold Macmillan reportedly murmured: 'Might we have a translation of that?'

A broad hint

Winston Churchill often used his wit and charm to get his way – but even he could not win every time. As the Second

World War neared its end, he was in Yalta with Joseph Stalin and Franklin D. Roosevelt. The purpose of the conference was, of course, to draw up an agreed map of the post-war world – but as the three leaders wrestled with these matters of international diplomacy, Churchill had set his heart upon a personal gift.

The British delegation was housed in the magnificent Alubka Palace, which looks out over the Black Sea, and Churchill had several times stood and admired a great marble statue of a lion in the grounds. It lay as if half-asleep, its head resting on its front paws, and it is not too much to suppose that the British Prime Minister had enough vanity to see something of himself in the magnificent creature.

In a suitably roundabout way, during a pause in the negotiations, Churchill raised the possibility of the statue being offered as a gift. Commenting on the fine craftsmanship and the noble bearing of the lion, he paused for a moment. He understood, he said, that there was a Russian tradition of offering the finest things in the country to show the sincerity of the welcome that was extended to an honoured guest.

But Stalin was too quick for him. 'Indeed,' he said. 'And the finest thing that we have in Russia is socialism.'

The lion stayed in Yalta.

A gift to an unknown beggar

Mohandas Karamchand Gandhi, the renowned Indian independence leader, was universally revered among hundreds of millions of Hindus as Mahatma Gandhi, or 'Great Soul' – and he retained an openhearted kindliness that transcended courtesy.

The story is still told in India of the day that he was being helped on to a train, clad only in his homespun *dhoti* and simple sandals. As the train moved off, one of his sandals slipped off his foot and on to the track below. Without pausing, Gandhi bent down, took the sandal off his other foot, and tossed it out of the train as well. His companions couldn't understand why he should have done such a thing, until he explained.

'Now, the poor man who finds the sandal I have lost will find another one as well, so he will have a pair to wear,' he said.

A regal gesture

As Ibn Saud, the first King of Saudi Arabia, became an old man, age and the wealth of his country's newly discovered oil wells meant that he travelled only in cars rather than by horse or camel – but he was delighted when, on a visit to the hot springs of the oasis town of Hofuf, a local dignitary offered him the gift of a handsome grey stallion.

Like his people, he valued the Arab tradition of generosity, but he also knew that it was important for him to repay the compliment. He summoned his vizier, and called for the massive leather-bound ledger in which were recorded details of the gifts he intended to bestow upon his subjects.

In it, he inscribed the name of the man who had given him the horse, and alongside wrote the sum of 300 riyals which, being considerably more than the horse was worth, would be a fitting way to mark his gratitude and demonstrate his own largesse in return. But unfortunately, as he wrote the nib of his pen caught slightly on the paper, sending a shower of tiny ink blots over the page. The Arabic symbol for a zero is a dot rather than a 0, and the accident had turned the king's 300 riyals into 300,000.

The vizier, commendably careful for his master's wealth, pointed out the error. The king studied the page carefully. 'I see that I have written 300,000 riyals, and that is what you must pay,' he said. 'It is the writing of my hand. Let no man say that the hand of Ibn Saud is more generous than his heart.'

The way of the world

One good friend, on holiday in Syria, was struck by the general friendliness and courtesy of the people. In Damascus, people would spot him in the street as a European, and smile broadly and say, 'Welcome to Syria'. Children would wave excitedly, and old men would look up from their hubble-bubble pipes with a smile.

No doubt they wanted to practise their English; after all, there are not many tourists in Syria – but the good humour and the welcome were clearly genuine.

Sometimes, however, courtesy may not be all it seems. On the same trip, my friend took a taxi with his wife, who worked for the BBC, and they were impressed again by the outspoken friendliness of the driver. What did they think of his country, he asked them, in perfect English. What were they going to see? And then suddenly, as they started to tell him about their experiences, he broke out in a passionate tirade against the government.

Ministers were corrupt, he said – 'Look, here is the special shop where only they can buy goods' – and the poor were cheated at every turn. The police were brutal and they took bribes – all charges which my friend and his wife were well aware had also been made by various international organisations. Then the taxi-driver stopped the car, and there were tears in his eyes.

'My heart is bursting,' he said. 'It is so good to be able to speak openly. My son' – and here he pulled a photograph of a little boy from his pocket – 'I hope my son will grow up in a better country than this.' He wouldn't take a fare, he said, because he had been so happy to be able to talk about his feelings, and it was only with difficulty that my friend persuaded him to take a 'present' for his son, which was about the cost of the journey plus a fair-sized tip.

It was a truly moving encounter for them, and they told the Syrian friend with whom they were staying all about it that night.

'Hmm,' she said. 'It's nice that he should be so interested in you. But you say you told him that you work for the BBC? Funny that a taxi driver should speak such perfect English. Most of them are informers for the secret police.'

So had my friend and his wife been speaking to a free-thinking parent who loved his son and yearned for freedom, or a cold, calculating and cynical secret police informer wanting to know what a couple of journalists were doing in Syria? He has never known.

THE SOCIAL WHIRL

Noblesse oblige is an interesting and unusual phrase; a reminder that social standing carries obligations as well as entitlements. If your rank gets you to the front of the queue, it implies you ought to be prepared to do something to earn the privilege.

It goes even further than the old line that all our mothers taught us about treating others in the way that we would expect to be treated: *noblesse oblige* means that we set our own high standards, and however other people may treat us, we will treat them with courtesy and consideration.

It's not always a popular idea; there are plenty of tales of pompous, self-important aristocrats whose only concern is that they should be shown the deference to which they think they should be entitled. At every level of society, we've all met the bores, bullies and buffoons who believe that the party is being held just so that they can show off and monopolise the floor.

But there are others stories of subtlety, kindness and good humour that deserve not to be forgotten. Here are a few of them – together with one or two to remind us of the prickly way in which people may sometimes fall short of the highest standards.

Confrontation on board *Britannia*

Maybe the best way to work out how one should treat one's guests is to imagine how the queen would handle any difficult situation. Royalists and republicans alike seem to agree that she never puts a foot wrong.

On one occasion, she was entertaining President Reagan and his wife at dinner as guests of honour on the royal yacht *Britannia*. In a startling break with royal protocol, she announced that she herself would serve the coffee, and dismissed the stewards. Most people served personally with their coffee by the queen would accept whatever was offered – but the president waved her away. 'No thanks. Do you have a decaff?' he asked airily.

The steward was recalled, and the president's order for decaffeinated coffee was sent off to the kitchens. But President Reagan hadn't finished. He reached out a hand and affectionately patted the queen on her bottom. 'Thanks for taking care of that,' he said.

The queen is a stickler for correct behaviour, and nobody, but nobody, touches her, ever. Aghast, the other guests waited for her response to this piece of trans-Atlantic *lèse-majesté*. Icy, angry or contemptuous, it was hard to imagine how an embarrassing incident could be avoided.

'That's perfectly all right, Mr President,' she smiled. And everyone breathed a sigh of relief.

Taking tea with the queen

Even at Buckingham Place, everything does not always go according to plan. When the queen entertained the victorious England World Cup rugby team for high tea – not being a drink that many of the players were particularly familiar with – the team's hooker Mark Regan was approached by a palace servant wearing scarlet livery with gold frogging on his coat and a tray in his hands.

'Earl Grey, sir?' he said.

Regan, taken slightly by surprise but determined to do the right thing, bowed slightly. 'Mark Regan, your lordship,' he replied smartly.

That, at least, is what Simon Shaw, another member of the team, says. And since he is 6ft 9in tall and weighs over 19 stone, few people argue with him.

Bomb? What bomb?

Sometimes courtesy may be about nothing more or less than refusing to be diverted from the matter in hand. If people have gathered for a particular purpose, it would be unpardonable rudeness to allow oneself to be distracted.

At the height of the Blitz, the Duke of Devonshire was presiding over a committee meeting at the exclusive Pratt's Club in London, which had been called to discuss the election of new members.

Halfway through the proceedings, there was a massive explosion nearby, bringing down the ceiling in a shower of plaster and extinguishing all the lights. After a few minutes, fresh lights were brought and the duke, slightly dishevelled and dusty, blinked around the committee table.

'I can't remember – did we elect the feller or not?' he inquired.

The perfect host

The statesman, financier and imperialist Cecil Rhodes is a controversial figure; remembered by some as a bully and a racist in Africa, and by others as the philanthropic founder of the Rhodes scholarships that have brought thousands of scholars from all over the world to Oxford University. One story frequently told about him, however, suggests that he was a man who knew how to be a host.

He had invited friends to dinner at his mansion in Kimberley, and they were all gathered in dinner jackets waiting for their host to appear. There was a nervous knock at the door and the last guest appeared – a young man who had just arrived by train, and who had no clothes other than the scruffy and travel-stained ones he was wearing. Mortified by his faux pas, he had just joined the others when Rhodes came into the room – wearing a disreputable old blue suit.

His servants had told him what had happened, and he had changed out of his dinner jacket in order to welcome his guests.

Deciding on a menu

Everyone has heard of the vast banquets of imperial Rome; of the grilled peacocks and roast ostriches; of the dormice dipped in honey and the slaves pouring wine from huge jars; and of the gluttonous patricians stuffing themselves until they vomited, and then stuffing themselves some more.

But as the lawyer, observer and inveterate letter-writer Pliny the Younger reminds us, it wasn't always like that.

In a letter to a young friend, Junius Avitus, a rising young politician to whom Pliny was a moral guide and mentor, he described his disgust at being entertained by a man who claimed to have found the best way to combine splendour with economy. He and Pliny had the best of everything; there was cheaper food and wine for the bulk of the guests and an even lower grade of provisions for the former slaves who were there with their masters.

Pliny was outraged by what he called 'this conjunction of self indulgence and meanness'. At his own dinners, all the guests were fed the same, he said. 'Every man whom I have treated as equal with myself by inviting him to dinner, I treat as an equal in every way,' he said.

'What?' asked his host, incredulously. 'Even the former slaves?'

'Even the former slaves,' said Pliny. 'On occasions like that, I see them as my guests and companions.'

The other man laughed, still not believing him. 'That must put you to huge expense,' he objected. But Pliny shook his head. 'Not at all. My guests and former slaves do not drink wine that I normally do – I drink the same wine that they do.'

This, said Pliny, was a lesson that young Avitus should bear in mind. If a man is wise enough to curb his own greed, he will not find it so very expensive to entertain his visitors as he does himself.

Maybe to twenty-first-century ears, he might occasionally sound a bit of a self-satisfied and prosy old bore – but it's not bad advice, all the same.

How to escape a bore …

One of the most common problems at a party is dealing with the person who just won't go away; the one who tells you the same story for a second or third time, the one who gets you in a corner and won't let you go, or the one who thinks that a conversation is carried on only with the mouth and not the ears as well. It's a problem that has probably existed for as long as people have talked to each other, and no one has come up with the perfect answer. But these three stories do at least show some of the ways people have tried to deal with it without being rude.

The poet Samuel Taylor Coleridge seems to have been, to put it politely, a difficult man to listen to. He, from time to time, used to give sermons at chapel services, and on one occasion asked his friend Charles Lamb whether he had heard him preach. 'My dear chap,' Lamb replied, 'I never heard you do anything else.'

Lamb also described how later – and maybe more kindly – he dealt with Coleridge's habit of holding him by the button of his coat and then, eyes closed and making languid gestures with his hand, starting on a rambling monologue that could sometimes go on for hours at a time:

> I saw that it was no use to break away, so … with my penknife I quietly severed the button from my coat and decamped. Five hours later and passing the same garden

on my way home, I heard Coleridge's voice and, looking in, there he was with closed eyes, the button in his fingers, and his right hand gently waving, just as when I left him.

The great Victorian actor Henry Irving suffered a rather more forceful rebuff. Chatting to Mark Twain, he embarked on a lengthy story, but paused after a few sentences to ask if Twain had heard it before. 'No, no,' said Twain. 'Definitely not.' Irving resumed the tale, and then, a few moments later, broke off again.

'Are you quite sure you haven't heard this earlier?'

'No,' said Twain, slightly more testily, and off Irving went again. This time, he had almost reached the climax of the story before he paused to ask the same question. It was too much for Twain. 'I can lie once,' he said. 'I can lie twice for courtesy's sake, but I draw the line there. I can't lie for a third time at any price. And anyway, I invented the story!'

Again, that may be of limited use as a guide to how one should behave. But the poet Robert Browning had a technique that anyone could copy to this day. Tried beyond endurance at a party by a bore who showed no signs of letting him escape, he gave him his most engaging smile. 'But my dear fellow,' he said, patting him on the elbow, 'this is too bad of me. I'm monopolising you.'

And off he went, free at last, and no unpleasantness caused. A lesson to us all.

…And how not to do it

Winston Churchill's son, Randolph, was sometimes said to have inherited his father's irascibility but none of his charm. Unsurprisingly perhaps, he provides an example of how *not* to get rid of a monopolising bore with style.

He is said to have been buttonholed late at night, as he tried to leave his club, by a fellow member who was well known for his long and tedious stories. Randolph listened for as long as his patience lasted – probably not very long – and then called over one of the club's servants.

'Listen to his Lordship's story until he has finished,' he said, and left.

The bulldog & the chicken

Sir Winston Churchill, like Oscar Wilde and George Bernard Shaw, is a man around whom stories gather. Many of them are about his biting wit or his growling surliness. When France's President Charles de Gaulle, for instance – with whom he was never the best of friends – told him that the French people saw him as the reincarnation of Joan of Arc, Churchill reminded him with a harrumph: 'We had to burn the last one!'

But the old bulldog could also be as charming as a puppy. Being served with cold chicken at a rather refined buffet in America, he asked his hostess, 'May I have some breast, please?'

Slightly taken aback, she replied: 'Mr Prime Minister, in this country, we usually ask for white meat or dark meat.'

Churchill – who was, of course, half American – apologised profusely, and the next day the lady received an orchid brought by a personal courier. With it was a note from the British Prime Minister: 'I would be honoured if you would pin this on your white meat.'

The prime minister's pyjamas

It is practically an article of faith today that 'the old days' were a quieter, gentler time, when people treated each other more kindly and the world – or at least part of it – was cushioned in courtesy and consideration. So here is a story that seems to prove it.

It's set among the glittering young things that Evelyn Waugh wrote about in his novels – indeed, he used this incident as the basis for a scene in his book *Vile Bodies*.

Two young aristocratic sisters, Lady Sibell and Lady Mary Lygon, aged 22 and 19, and daughters of the immensely wealthy Lord Beauchamp, had spent the night partying in their white Norman Hartnell dresses. Then, like many young people before and since, they arrived home in the small hours to find themselves locked out. The doors of their father's Belgrave Square house were bolted, and the night footman – admittedly not a feature of most families – could not be woken.

So what could be more natural than that they should turn to an old family friend to ask for a bed for the night, or what was left of it? They hurried round to the friend's house, which was nearby, and summoned the night porter. He in turn called his master and mistress; and the Prime Minister of the United Kingdom, Right Honourable Stanley Baldwin, KG, PC, and his wife Lucy appeared in the hallway of 10 Downing Street in their nightclothes – Baldwin sporting a fetching pair of striped silk pyjamas beneath his dressing gown.

Of course the girls would be made welcome, Baldwin smiled courteously, and they were ushered off to their rooms. In the morning the prime minister made time to ring Lord Beauchamp – no doubt urging him not to be too cross with his wayward daughters – and asked him to send a maid round with some ordinary clothes for them. 'Balderdash and poppycock!' was the crusty old peer's reply; the girls had to walk home through the bustling streets of London in their full evening dress.

So far, so charming, even allowing for the fact that this little adventure took place in a world to which the vast mass of people had no access. The story seems as quaint and dated as a sepia photograph, although in fact, it's not so distant as it appears – Lady Sibell died only in 2005, at the age of 98.

But it may be worth remembering that the old days could be every bit as vicious, scandalous and unforgiving as our own times. Lord Beauchamp ended his days exiled and in disgrace, after a homosexual scandal that reached right to the top of British society; the two carefree young girls were bitterly estranged from their parents; and Baldwin spent his old age criticised and reviled by a nation that was bitter about his pre-war support for the appeasement policy.

But the image of the prime minister in his pyjamas, standing with his wife at the door of 10 Downing Street to welcome two young girls who were stranded and in trouble, remains as a reminder of the simpler, more caring time that we like to believe used to be.

The first to enter & the last to leave

In early May 1897 horrified newspaper readers all over the world were faced with the details of a horrific fire in Paris' *rue Jean Goujon*, in which scores of people had died. The fire had raged through the city's Great Charity Bazaar in minutes, apparently after a curtain caught fire while a film was being shown. Roofs of blazing tar had collapsed on to the heads of the workers, the exhibitors and the high society patrons of the event as they tried to flee.

The exact number of dead has never been established – some contemporary estimates were as high as 200, among them some of the most glittering names in Parisian society. Baroness Elizabeth St Martin; the Comtesse St Perrier; Madame Flores, the wife of the Spanish consul;

the Marchioness de Gallifet – the list of dead echoing the invitation list to one of the capital's most exclusive events. The bazaar had been planned as a massive event at which members of the French aristocracy would raise money for charity, and it had been widely supported.

But the highest ranking name of all was that of Sophie Charlotte, Duchesse d'Alençon, the sister of the Empress of Austria and the Queen of Sicily. The newspapers revealed that her engagement ring, inscribed with her name and that of her husband had been found; so had a silver watch, attached to a gold brooch that she was known to have been wearing. It was several days before her badly burned body was found.

Fireman, ordinary workmen, servants and tradesmen died in the blaze alongside the aristocrats – and struggled alongside them, too, to bring people out of the flames to safety. There were many tales of heroism that day, some of them tragic like the father who pulled his wife from the flames and then died with his daughter in his arms as he struggled to carry her to safety too. Some of them had happy endings. But it was only a few days later that the story of the death of the Duchesse d'Alençon began to emerge.

A group of workmen from a nearby site had fought their way through the flames to where the duchess' stall had been, at the far end of the bazaar. They had tried to persuade her to let them take her to safety on a nearby patch of waste ground, but she had refused; the girls who had been working with her on the charity stalls should be rescued first, she said.

'Because of my position, I was the first person to enter here,' she told them. 'Because of my position, I shall be the last to leave.'

A harsh lesson

There are, it seems, exceptions to the rule about making your guests feel at home. Some sins appear to be just too heinous to overlook. Take the grand society lady who saw, to her horror, that a young girl had lit a cigarette as the soup course was being cleared away. With a melodramatic clearing of her throat, and a stare that would have stripped paint at 30 yards, she rose to her feet.

'We appear to have finished,' she said in a ringing voice, and led her guests from the room.

Dinner was over – and the mortified young girl probably never smoked during a meal again.

An old-fashioned way of business

Since its foundation in the eighteenth century, Coutts and Company has enjoyed an unrivalled reputation as the bank of high society, offering its services to the queen and generations of the royal family. This relationship began in the 1760s, when George III opened an account with Thomas Coutts, one of the two Scottish brothers who founded the bank.

Coutts had been dining with some of his fellow financiers, and heard one of them telling a story about refusing a loan to a certain nobleman who needed £30,000 – something over £2 million in today's money. Coutts said nothing, but later that night went to the peer's house and left a message to say that if his lordship were to call the following morning, he might learn something to his advantage.

Intrigued, the nobleman was ushered into Coutts' offices the next day. The banker took a bundle of banknotes from a drawer, and counted out £31,000 on his desk. 'I believe this is what you require,' he said. Astonished, the peer asked what security would be required for the loan. 'I shall be more than satisfied with your lordship's note of hand,' Coutts replied.

This may not be a style of banking that would be acceptable these days, but it resulted in the peer opening a large account with Coutts' bank shortly afterwards, when he sold an estate – and also led to his recommending the bank a short while later to King George.

Family embarrassment

A wise man once said that a good host should make his guests feel at home even when he wishes that they were

– but for the queen, the problem is sometimes quite the reverse. She has to make her hosts feel at ease, even when they are the president and First Lady of the United States.

In November 1985 President Gerald Ford and his wife Betty entertained the queen and Prince Philip to dinner. Their 23-year-old son, Jack, was dressing for the formal introductions when he realised that he had lost the studs for his dress shirt. He just had time to rush to his father's room to borrow some, and so shirt unfastened, hair tousled, and in his stockinged feet, he dashed down the corridor and into the lift – to find his parents with their royal guests already there.

Mrs Ford began to introduce her son and apologise for his appearance, but the queen stopped her. 'I have one at home just like that,' she smiled.

A noble restraint

In his diaries, the British theatre critic James Agate (1877–1947) recalled lunching with a duke at the latter's house in London in the 1930s. A well-known and much admired film actress of the day had also been invited. One o'clock arrived, and there was still no sign of the actress; nor had she arrived an hour later, by which time small talk was flagging and everyone was probably pie-eyed on sherry. Eventually, at 2.30 p.m., the butler answered the door to admit, in a cloud of 'Darlings!', the tardy guest, followed by her maid, who was struggling beneath a pile of packages and boxes.

Rushing to kiss the duke, the new arrival said breathlessly, 'Darling! I am *so* sorry if I'm just the teeniest bit late, but I simply *had* to buy a chandelier!'

At which the duke, detaching himself from her embrace, fixed his gaze on the ceiling and said quietly to himself, 'I once knew a chap who bought a chandelier *after* luncheon ...'

A fine line

For visitors to the houses of the rich, famous and aristocratic, there is often a fine line to be drawn between courtesy and abject sycophancy. During the nineteenth century the wealthy landowner Lord Crewe had his palatial home, Crewe Hall in Cheshire, extensively rebuilt after a fire. Part of the £150,000 project – worth some £10 million at today's rates – was the reconstruction of a magnificent carved Jacobean staircase which swept down into the central hall.

He was known to be justifiably proud of his house, and particularly of his staircase – so when an elderly lady who was visiting slipped on the top step and tumbled the full length of the stairs, there was considerable consternation.

As she lay stunned at the foot of the carved and gilded oak newel posts, her husband dashed forward to speak to his lordship. 'Oh, Lord Crewe,' he said, 'I do hope my wife hasn't damaged your beautiful staircase.'

Putting a name to a face

During the 1920s Douglas Fairbanks' Beverly Hills mansion, Pickfair, was the acknowledged centre of Hollywood social life. Apart from a glittering array of film stars and writers, guests at the parties given by Fairbanks and his wife Mary Pickford included a number of the crowned heads of Europe and several members of the English aristocracy.

One day, Fairbanks was driving home when he saw a figure he vaguely recognised walking along the road in the heat. He stopped the car to offer the man a lift, registering his cut-glass English accent, expensively styled suit and aristocratic bearing – but still struggling to put a name to the face.

As they drove along they chatted about the challenges of owning and maintaining a twenty-two room mansion, with its fabulous art collection and its extensive grounds, and Fairbanks' passenger made several incisive and approving comments about the organisation of the whole Pickfair estate. Clearly, he was accustomed to living in some style; he must, Fairbanks concluded, be one of his recent aristocratic guests.

Still unwilling to face the embarrassment of admitting that he could not remember his friend's name, he invited him in for a drink, and snatched the opportunity of asking his secretary what the man was called. 'He's obviously a lord, but I can't remember his name,' he said.

'Don't know the guy's name, Mr Fairbanks,' came the laconic reply. 'But he's the English butler you fired last month for drunkenness.'

A marriage proposal

During the First World War, the Buckinghamshire estate of Cliveden – later notorious as the stately home at the heart of the Profumo scandal – was used as a Red Cross hospital for wounded soldiers from the trenches.

Cliveden's chatelaine Nancy Astor, American-born wife of Viscount Astor, was then in her mid-thirties, and worked among the soldiers as a nurse, tending their wounds. One day a young Canadian soldier, who had been lying unconscious, awoke to find her gazing down at him. Entranced by her beauty, he murmured: 'You're the kind of person I'd like to take back to Canada as my wife.' (Being a soldier, he may well have made other suggestions as well, but whoever passed on the original story limited them to this tentative proposal of marriage.)

Viscountess Astor smiled down at him. 'Let me think it over for a day or so,' she said.

A few days later, one of the other patients told the rapidly recovering soldier the name of the nurse he had flirted with. The next time he saw her, he apologised abjectly, covered in confusion.

Her response? 'I haven't had such a compliment for a long time!'

Invitation to dinner

A truly generous host will ignore the rudeness of his guest, and make him feel at home however bad his behaviour has been – but courtesy is not always what it seems. This cautionary tale is told by the Victorian painter, W.P. Frith, in his autobiography.

Frith says that a distant cousin of his made a bet that he would gain entrance to the famously beautiful private gardens at Fonthill Abbey, the Wiltshire home of the writer William Beckford. Beckford, author of the gothic horror novel *Vathek*, was reputed to be a surly recluse who would not tolerate intrusions on his privacy.

Frith's cousin slipped into the park at Fonthill, through a gate that had been carelessly left open in the high stone walls that surrounded it, and was leaning on the second wall that separated the park from the abbey gardens when he was approached by a gardener. Far from throwing him out, the gardener offered to give him a tour of the grounds – and then, astonishingly, invited the young intruder into the abbey itself to look at Mr Beckford's fabled collections of books and paintings. Finally, seeing it was late in the afternoon, he insisted that he should stay for dinner – and when the young man demurred, the gardener declared that he was William Beckford himself.

The food and drink were magnificent, and Beckford's conversation fascinating. His guest hung on every word of his stories of Italian travel; his meetings with aristocrats, writers and artists; his philosophical thoughts; and his views on art and music. Surely, he thought, Beckford's reputation as a man who hated company was a gross libel.

And then, on the stroke of eleven, the famous author got up and left the room. The young man waited for him to return … and waited. He must have dozed off, because he was suddenly aware of the footman putting out the lights. Mr Beckford, the footman told him as he led him to the great oak front door, had gone to bed.

'This is very strange,' he said. 'I expected Mr Beckford back again. I wished to thank him for his hospitality.'

'Mr Beckford ordered me to present his compliments to you, sir,' replied the footman. 'I am to say that as you found your way into Fonthill Abbey without permission, you may find your way out again as best you can. And he hopes you will take care to avoid the bloodhounds that are let loose in the garden every night.'

And with that the door slammed shut. Hearing the baying of the bloodhounds, the young man climbed the first tree he could find and spent a long and miserable night there until daybreak when he escaped. He had won his bet – but, he said, 'not for fifty million times the amount would I again pass such a night as I did at Fonthill Abbey.'

SPORTING GESTURES

Any dedicated sportsman will tell you that there's no point in playing the game if you don't play to win. Nice guys, they say, always come last – and there are plenty of stories to show that gamesmanship, cheating and unsportsmanlike behaviour can be effective. But as long as sport has been played, there have also been people who have wanted to win, but not at any price. The tradition of courtesy and generosity in sport is a long and honourable one, and these stories demonstrate that it knows no distinction between gentlemen and players, or between amateurs and professionals. Whether they are amateur athletes from a bygone age, or Premiership footballers in our own time, there are dedicated competitors who clearly believe that there are some things – not many of them, perhaps, but still some things – that are more important than winning. And the strange thing is they often do win in the end. Nice guys, in fact, do sometimes come first.

Walking the walk

Adam Gilchrist, wicket-keeper batsman for the Australian cricket team until 2008, was an unusual cricketer. It's not just that he played international cricket for twelve years, and not even that he's generally considered to have been one of the best wicket-keepers in history.

Gilchrist used to walk.

That means that when he was batting, if he knew he'd nicked the ball to the wicket-keeper, he would set off for the pavilion without waiting for the umpire to make a decision. Walking is a sporting admission by a batsman that he's out that's often seen as the mark of a gentleman in cricket – and it is increasingly rare in the international game. Most batsmen stand their ground and thank their lucky stars if the umpire makes a mistake in their favour.

In his book *Walking to Victory*, Gilchrist described a World Cup semi-final match against Sri Lanka in 2003 where he knew he'd given a thick edge to the wicket-keeper. The Sri Lankans appealed, but the umpire shook his head, meaning that he didn't think Gilchrist had touched the ball, and so was not out.

But Gilchrist knew better. 'The voice in my head was emphatic. Go. Walk. And I did,' he said:

Of course, the guys back in the viewing room were a bit stunned at what I'd done. Flabbergasted, really, that I'd do it in a World Cup semi. While I sat there, thinking about it and being asked about it, I kept going back to the fact that, well, at the end of the day, I had been honest with myself. I felt it was time that players made a stand to take back responsibility for the game.

Walking isn't just a demonstration of sportsmanship and honesty – it's an act of courtesy to the opposing team, and especially to the umpire. After his action in the Sri Lanka match, Gilchrist says, he was worried that he might have embarrassed umpire Rudi Koertzen, who had initially given him not out – but when he caught his eye as the teams took the field at the beginning of the next innings, Koertzen gave a little nod and a brief clap of his hands in silent appreciation of what he'd done.

None of this means that Gilchrist is pious or self-satisfied. Asked some years later whether he would walk if he nicked a ball to the wicket-keeper in the final Test Match of a series, with Australia needing a few runs to win and just one wicket left, he paused, puffed out his cheeks, and gave the question a moment's thought.

'Ah, mate,' he said. 'In those circumstances, I wouldn't be nicking the ball behind in the first place.'

A true champion

Courtesy is what makes the cliché true: sport really can be less about winning and more about taking part. Matthew Syed, once an international table tennis player and now a respected sports journalist, tells a story about the greatest victory of his sporting career, against the then world champion, Jörgen Persson of Sweden.

It was the tense climax of a hard-fought match, he said in his column in *The Times*. The score was 19–19 in the deciding fifth game – with both players trying to qualify for the 1996 Olympics – and then, one of Syed's shots seemed to miss the end of the table. Point to Persson.

But what Persson had seen was that the ball had actually grazed the edge of the table, only by a whisker, but enough to mean that the point should have been Syed's. No one else had seen it; not umpires, not spectators and certainly not Syed.

The stakes could not have been higher, and there could have been no one to blame Persson if he had simply kept quiet and taken the point and probably won the game, and hence the match.

'Persson did not hesitate, not for an instant, nodding in my direction, signalling what had happened and turning the scoreboard in my favour,' says Syed:

> I was so surprised, so touched, that I said something that still echoes in my ears today: 'Are you sure?'

'Yes, I am sure,' he said.

Afterwards, having won the match, I approached Persson and thanked him for his integrity. 'I wanted to win,' he said. 'But not if it meant winning like that.'

The greatest sporting encounters ever?

It is possible to see the history of polar exploration as one of scientific advance, or even as part of the imperialism with which western nations seized great tracts of the world for themselves. But occasionally, the polar adventure was a straightforward race between rival expeditions; and it was always a contest between brave men and the elements. Maybe the journeys to the North and South Poles have been, in essence, a series of the greatest sporting encounters ever.

There have been stories of incredible achievement, such as that of the Norwegian explorer Roald Amundsen, who won the race against Robert Falcon Scott's British expedition in January 1912. Scott himself told a story of tragedy and nobility, with his account of the self sacrifice of Captain Lawrence Oates, who famously walked to his death in a polar storm rather than slow down his colleagues in their doomed attempt to reach safety. Oates' memorial, erected near the scene of his death by the rescuers who eventually found the bodies of his companions, described him as 'a very gallant gentleman'. His reported last words, 'I am just going outside, and I may be some time', exemplified the sense of chivalry and self-effacement implicit in that description.

And Scott's own words, left in his journal as he lay dying in his tent, also deserve to be remembered for their dignity: 'We took risks, we knew we took them; things have come out against us, and therefore we have no cause for complaint, but bow to the will of Providence, determined still to do our best to the last.'

But there has also been comedy in the frozen wastes of the Antarctic. Sir Edgeworth David was a distinguished Australian geologist who accompanied the explorer Ernest Shackleton on the expedition of 1907–09, which travelled further south than anyone had managed before. During the expedition Shackleton's physicist, Douglas Mawson, was working in his tent when he heard a cry from outside. It was Sir Edgeworth.

'Are you very busy?' he called.

Mawson, who was correlating some data and did not want to be disturbed, replied rather testily, 'Yes, I am. What is it?'

There was a pause. 'Are you really *very* busy?' came the call.

'Yes, actually,' Mawson snapped back. It is seldom a good idea to interrupt a physicist while he is working on his data. 'What is it that you want?'

There was another short pause, and then the impeccably mannered Sir Edgeworth shouted back apologetically, 'Well, it's just that I'm down a crevasse, and I'm not sure that I can hang on much longer!'

How things can be

It's more than seventy years since he won his four Olympic gold medals and more than thirty years since he died, but Jesse Owens remains one of the most evocative names in Olympic history. His triumphs in the 1936 Berlin Games – where he won gold medals in the 100 metres, the 200 metres, the long jump and the 100-metre relay – challenged the unshakable belief of his Nazi hosts in the superiority of white men over black, angered Hitler and delighted most of the rest of the world.

Enough went on in public to justify the respect and fame that his name still enjoys – although in the years immediately following his triumph he went home to face a climate of racial prejudice in the US, eke out a living as a petrol pump attendant and eventually file for bankruptcy. But in private, Owens' long jump victory was the setting for an inspirational story of sportsmanship and human decency that transcended Nazi ideology.

Owens was competing against a blonde German hero, Carl Ludwig 'Luz' Long, who was widely expected to take the gold. During the competition, the two struck up a friendship that lasted for years. Some unconfirmed reports suggest that Long even helped his rival by marking the right take-off point for him when Owens, facing possible elimination from the competition, had to take a crucial qualifying jump. That may or may not be true – but what is known is that, after Owens' victory, when Hitler had stormed out of the stadium rather than present the gold medal to a black runner, Long, the silver medalist, was the first to offer his congratulations.

'It took a lot of courage for him to befriend me in front of Hitler. You can melt down all the medals and cups I have, and there wouldn't be a plating on the 24 carat friendship I felt for Luz Long at that moment,' Owens told reporters afterwards.

Because of the war the two men never met again, but they exchanged letters. Seven years later, Long – not a member of the Nazi Party, but a soldier in the German army – wrote to his old rival:

> My heart tells me this will be the last letter I write … If it is so, I ask you something. It is for you to go to Germany when this war is done, someday find my son and tell him about his father. Tell him, Jesse, what times were like when we were not separated by war … I am saying, tell him how things can be between men on this earth.

It was Long's last letter. Shortly afterwards he was killed during the German invasion of Sicily. Owens not only fulfilled his request, and maintained a regular correspondence with Long's son Kai, but also stood by Kai's side in the 1960s as best man at his wedding. He did indeed tell him, and a whole generation, how things can be between men on this earth.

No dumbbells here

Bear Bryant was a famous American college football coach during the fifties, sixties and seventies, who was noted for his tough, no-nonsense approach towards his players. One of the stars who played for him – 'the greatest athlete I ever coached,' Bryant said – was the great quarterback Joe Namath.

The coach was a strict disciplinarian, the player known for speaking his mind: it could have been a recipe for conflict. Instead, it showed that courtesy and affection aren't necessarily incompatible with a sense of humour.

On one occasion, Bryant was growling at his University of Alabama squad about the need for self-respect on and off the field. 'This is a class operation. I want your shoes to be shined, I want you to have a tie on, to get your hair cut, and to keep a crease in your pants. I also want you to go to class,' he said. 'I don't want no dumbbells on this team. If there is a dumbbell in this room, I want him to stand up.'

Nobody moved. You just didn't take on Bear Bryant in that way. Then, slowly and deliberately, Namath rose to his feet.

Bryant looked at him in surprise for a second. 'Joe, how come you're standing up? You ain't dumb.'

'Well,' said Namath, 'it's just that I hate like the devil to see you standing up there all by yourself, Coach.'

The right thing to do

Paulo di Canio, the Italian football star who played in the English Premiership from 1997 to 2004, is nobody's idea of a pussycat. In 1998, for instance, he served an eleven-match suspension for pushing over the referee who sent him off while playing for Sheffield Wednesday against Arsenal.

And yet, among professional footballers, his name is forever linked with one of the most striking displays of instinctive sportsmanship seen in the modern game.

In December 2000, di Canio was playing for West Ham against Everton. The match was well into injury time, with the teams level at one goal all, when a cross came over from the right wing to di Canio, waiting in the Everton penalty area. There was an open goal; all he had to do was bring the ball down and put it in the net, and his team would take the valuable three points for a win away from home.

Instead, he caught the ball in his arms, conceding an automatic free kick, and gesturing towards the Everton goalkeeper, Paul Gerrard, lying in agony on the ground several yards away. In fact, Gerrard had twisted his knee, but di Canio believed he could have broken his leg. It was more important, he thought, that his fellow professional should get urgent medical attention than that he should score the winning goal.

'I saw the goalkeeper doubled over. I saw his knee twisted in the wrong direction,' he said. 'It seemed like the right thing to do, but I didn't really think about it. A serious injury to any professional is far worse than losing two points.'

The Everton crowd gave di Canio an immediate standing ovation; his manager, Harry Redknapp, described the incident as 'sportsmanship of the highest merit'; FIFA, football's international governing body, presented him with its special Fair Play Award. But the player himself was bemused by all the attention he achieved.

'I am not a saint, just like I was not a killer two years ago with the referee when I did something wrong,' he said. 'During the game, the opposition is my enemy. But when they are injured, they are my colleagues and I must help them.'

Sports fans who want to be grumpy might say that the fact that such an act of sportsmanship should have received so much attention simply shows how low standards usually are. But di Canio's own words – 'It seemed like the right thing to do, but I didn't really think about it' – surely sum up something very important about the way sport should be played.

A great Olympian

There's no reason why the courtesy of great sportsmen should be extended only to their competitors; no reason, in fact, why courtesy should be extended only to human beings. Take the case of the great Australian Olympian Bobby Pearce – Henry Robert Pearce, to give him his full name. Pearce was an oarsman who won gold in the single sculls event at the 1928 Amsterdam Olympics, and successfully defended his title four years later in Los Angeles, going on later in his career to become World Champion from 1933 to 1938.

In Amsterdam, Pearce stormed through his heats on the city's Stoten Canal, beating the opposition with several lengths to spare. In the quarter final, the same pattern seemed to be repeating itself, with Pearce building up a commanding lead over his French opponent Victor Saurin.

But then, glancing over his shoulder, he saw a mother duck with a small train of ducklings behind her swimming directly into his path. Pearce leant on his oars, bringing his boat to a shuddering stop as the family of ducks passed serenely in front of him. Saurin, meanwhile, who had no idea what had happened, caught up with him and powered past, pulling away to a lead of five lengths. But with the ducks safely out of the way, Pearce started rowing again and won the race, going on through the semi-final and the final to take the gold with a new Olympic record – surely one of the most unusual victories in Olympic history.

Count me out

On 14 May 1938 the England football team played Germany at Berlin's *Olympiastadion*. Was it, as several newspapers have suggested, the most shameful moment in British sporting history? Or was it simply the members of a national team showing courtesy and civility towards their hosts?

Britain's ambassador to Germany, Sir Neville Henderson, had no doubts when he advised the team on how they should behave. 'When I go to see Herr Hitler, I give him the Nazi salute, because that is the normal courtesy expected,' he said. The Football Association officials with the team agreed – and that is how photographs came to be taken of an England football team standing with their arms raised in the Nazi salute as the band played *Deutschland über alles*. Among them was possibly the country's greatest ever football hero, Sir Stanley Matthews.

In fact, Hitler was not at the match – but for some of the players, it was a defining moment. England's captain, the Arsenal fullback Eddie Hapgood, later served in the Royal Air Force. 'I've been V-bombed in Brussels before the Rhine crossing, and bombed and rocketed in London; I've been in a shipwreck, a train crash, and inches short of a plane accident,' he said later. 'But the worst moment of my life, and the one I would not willingly go through again, was giving the Nazi salute in Berlin.'

The Football Association secretary, Stanley Rous, couldn't see what the fuss was about. The players, he said, 'no doubt saw it as a bit of fun'.

In fact, at least one of them, even at the time, certainly didn't. Stan Cullis, one of the defensive line-up alongside Hapgood and the youngest member of the team at just 22, gave a brisk, no-nonsense reply to the idea of the salute. 'Count me out,' he said – and they did, dropping him from the team.

It was a great night for England, who thrashed Germany 6–3. But perhaps as Cullis got older – he was 85 when he died in 2001, after a long and honourable career at Wolverhampton as both player and manager – he would look back on that match as the international cap he was glad he never got.

Indeed, there may be ways to play with tyrants and make a point. In 1974 the British Lions rugby team set off on a controversial tour of apartheid South Africa. Some players who would have been in the party had stayed at home and opted not to go on the tour; some were there to see for themselves what apartheid meant; others on the tour believed sincerely that sport and politics should not mix. Some, perhaps, didn't care anyway.

But the South Africans, terrified at the prospect of international sporting boycotts, were delighted to see them. A television reporter, no doubt bearing in mind the stereotype of a rugby player as a hard drinking, hard partying knucklehead who liked nothing better than a good sing-song, asked on air what was the Lions' team song.

'It's a song by the Specials,' came the reply. 'It's called *Free Nelson Mandela.*'

1 MONT

FREE
READING

at
www.ForgottenBooks.com

By purchasing this book you are eligible for one month membership to ForgottenBooks.com, giving you unlimited access to our entire collection of over 1,000,000 titles via our web site and mobile apps.

To claim your free month visit:

www.forgottenbooks.com/free175735

ISBN 978-0-265-24613-9
PIBN 10175735

THE SHORT COURSE SERIES

THE PSALM OF PSALMS

GENERAL PREFACE

THE title of the present series is a sufficient indication of its purpose. Few preachers, or congregations, will face the long courses of expository lectures which characterised the preaching of the past, but there is a growing conviction on the part of some that an occasional short course, of six or eight connected studies on one definite theme, is a necessity of their mental and ministerial life. It is at this point the projected series would strike in. It would suggest to those who are mapping out a scheme of work for the future a variety of subjects which might possibly be utilised in this way.

The appeal, however, will not be restricted to ministers or preachers. The various volumes will meet the needs of laymen and

General Preface

Sabbath-school teachers who are interested in a scholarly but also practical exposition of Bible history and doctrine. In the hands of office-bearers and mission-workers the "Short Course Series" may easily become one of the most convenient and valuable of Bible helps.

It need scarcely be added that while an effort has been made to secure, as far as possible, a general uniformity in the scope and character of the series, the final responsibility for the special interpretations and opinions introduced into the separate volumes, rests entirely with the individual contributors.

A detailed list of the authors and their subjects will be found at the close of each volume.

Volumes already Published

A Cry for Justice: A Study in Amos.
 By Prof. JOHN E. McFADYEN, D.D.

The Beatitudes.
 By Rev. ROBERT H. FISHER, D.D.

The Lenten Psalms.
 By the EDITOR.

The Psalm of Psalms.
 By Prof. JAMES STALKER, D.D.

The Song and the Soil.
 By Prof. W. G. JORDAN, D.D.

The Higher Powers of the Soul.
 By Rev. GEORGE M'HARDY, D.D.

PRICE 60 CENTS NET PER VOLUME

CHARLES SCRIBNER'S SONS

The Short Course Series

EDITED BY

Rev. JOHN ADAMS, B.D.

THE
PSALM OF PSALMS

BEING AN EXPOSITION OF THE
TWENTY-THIRD PSALM

BY THE

Rev. JAMES STALKER, M.A., D.D.,

PROFESSOR OF CHURCH HISTORY IN THE UNITED FREE COLLEGE
ABERDEEN

NEW YORK
CHARLES SCRIBNER'S SONS
1913

TO

T. O.

CONTENTS

———+———

THE Twenty-third Psalm is the nightingale among the Psalms. It is small, of a homely feather, singing shyly out of obscurity ; but it has filled the air of the whole world with melodious joy, greater than the heart can conceive. Blessed be the day on which that Psalm was born !

HENRY WARD BEECHER.

INTRODUCTION

INTRODUCTION

THE Decalogue, the Aaronic Blessing and the Twenty-third Psalm in the Old Testament, and the Beatitudes, the Lord's Prayer and the Apostolic Benediction in the New, with perhaps two or three other passages of similar calibre, are the best-known portions of Holy Writ. They were learned by us at a mother's knee, or at least from our earliest instructors; and they are all of sufficient substance to stand constant repetition, as solid gold is only brightened by frequent rubbing. To generations and centuries of men such scriptures have ministered "doctrine, reproof, correction, instruction in righteousness"; and, though they are the earliest efforts of memory, they will reward the maturest ponderings of the human mind. The Twenty-third Psalm, in

3

particular, ever since it sprang into existence from the inspired genius of its author, has served to express the experience of the pious ; and the modern man can measure his own progress and attainment by the extent to which he can make its sentiments his own. Not only, however, will the venerable words measure attainment, but they will stimulate it and awaken higher aspiration. Hence the psalm is worthy to be studied verse by verse and line by line.

I. Authorship.

There was a time, not very long ago, when any psalm might be quoted as a psalm of David. We have now reached a stage when it would be denied by experts of a certain class that even a single psalm can be proved to have proceeded from the Bard of Bethlehem. The one extreme is, however, as untenable as the other. When the controversy about such subjects first broke out in the Church with which I am connected, I remember a minister of saintliness and learn-

Introduction

ing declaring that for him the Fifty-first Psalm would lose all its virtue if it were not from the pen of David; and some may be inclined to say the same about this Twenty-third Psalm. I should not like to say this peremptorily about any piece in the Psalter; and in general I like to think of the Psalms as proceeding from a large number and variety of voices spread at intervals over the pre-Christian centuries. But, on the other hand, when the attribution of a psalm to some known personage, or its connection with some recorded event, throws light on the whole composition, and is not inconsistent with anything in the text, it seems to me to be extinguishing the light not to take advantage of this circumstance.

Now, the reasons for believing this Twenty-third Psalm to be a legacy bequeathed to the people of God by King David are very strong indeed, and the assumption that he is the author throws light on every verse.

First, it lies on the surface that the relation of God to His people is here compared to the relation of a shepherd to his sheep;

The Psalm of Psalms

and of this David could speak from experience, as he had been a shepherd. Indeed, the suggestion has not infrequently been made that he may have composed this lyric whilst as a ruddy youth he was watching his flocks on the pastures of his father Jesse. On the other hand, however, it has been observed with truth that the experience here described is not that of a stripling or beginner, but of one mature in the life divine, who has had experience of all forms of guidance, in vicissitude as well as rest, in gloom as well as sunshine. But, even if the psalm was composed in old age or at least maturity, as it probably was, the sweet singer could make use of the experiences of his youth, which he could not have forgotten. At that time he had been a model shepherd, loving his flock and loved by them ; and in the psalm the entire life of a sheep under a good shepherd is employed as an image or parable of a human life led under the guidance and protection of God.

But it may not have been noted by some readers, often as they have read and sung

6

Introduction

this psalm, that, in the second half of it, we are away from the image of the sheep altogether, and that another image is being developed. When, at v. 5, it is said, " Thou preparest a table before me in the presence of mine enemies ; Thou anointest my head with oil ; my cup runneth over," it is obvious that the words are put not into the mouth of a sheep, but into that of a guest, and that the person addressed is no longer conceived of as a shepherd, but as a host or entertainer. The table spread, the head anointed, the cup full to overflowing are obvious features of a banquet ; and the idea is, that he who has God for his friend enjoys a continual feast, where everything is in abundance and everything is of the best. The same cheerful image is kept up in the closing verse—" Goodness and mercy shall follow me all the days of my life ; and I will dwell in the house of the Lord for ever." The favourite is not only to be a guest, but one who abides in the house for ever—that is, a son.

The point to be observed is, that this

The Psalm of Psalms

second image agrees, as well as does the first, with the experience of David. If, during the first half of his life, he was a shepherd, he was, during the second half, a king; and one of the duties of a king is hospitality. Indeed, this trait is mentioned again and again in the history as characteristic of David's mature life; and what a fascination he exercised as a host may be inferred from the offer of two of his braves to risk their lives in order to procure what he wanted, when he expressed a desire to taste a draught of water from the Well of Bethlehem. To his guests he could supply not only the good things of the table, but, with his musical gifts, the feast of reason and the flow of soul. If David was a model shepherd at one period of life, he was a model entertainer at another; and this experience also supplied him with the means of illustrating both the behaviour of God to men and the attitude of men to God.

We shall see afterwards why it was that David found the image of the shepherd insufficient, and had to add that of the royal

Introduction

entertainer. But, in the meantime, we perceive how natural it was that he should employ both figures of speech. I do not deny that another poet might have hit upon the same combination without having had either experience in his own case. But to have had the double experience in the same lifetime must have been a very rare thing. It certainly adds to the value of the psalm if we assume that the sweet singer was speaking from experience in both the beginning and the end of it. There is a life-likeness which supports this view; and, though it would be of no use to affirm dogmatically the Davidic authorship, we shall assume this throughout.

II. APPLICATION.

An eccentric professor, under whom I studied at college, used to say that the most important word in a text may be the one after the last; and it is certainly true that the message of no Old Testament passage is exhausted when it has been interpreted by the mere analysis of the words and their applica-

The Psalm of Psalms

tion to the original situation. The first duty of an interpreter is to find out what the writer meant to convey at the moment when he wrote ; but the words may suggest far more to a Christian reader. Of this a remarkable instance has often struck me : in the Thirty-first Psalm a saintly singer says, "Into thine hand I commit my spirit" ; but our Saviour, in quoting the words on the cross, prefaced them with the word "Father," thus placing on them His own distinctive signature ; and St. Stephen, in adopting them as his dying words, actually addressed them to the Saviour Himself, saying, "Lord Jesus, receive my spirit." This indicates how wide may be the scope of legitimate Christian application.

The principle applies to our Psalm also, which is a fine example of how the beautiful and profound passages of the Old Testament become far more beautiful and far more profound when read in the light of the New.

The image of the Good Shepherd, applied in the Old Testament to God, is applied in the New Testament to Christ ; it is especially

Introduction

applied by Jesus to Himself, as when He says, "The good shepherd giveth his life for the sheep." David might have introduced this feature into the Twenty-third Psalm; because, as we know from the account he gave of himself at his first interview with King Saul, there were more occasions than one when he risked his life for the flock. He omitted it; but the Son of David could not omit it, because this was to be His most characteristic act; "for the Son of man came not to be ministered unto but to minister, and to give his life a ransom for many." Some in our day are teaching that the supreme and final message of Jesus was trust in Providence—faith that the divine will, whatever it may be, is best. That is a priceless lesson; but it had been amply taught long before the Incarnation. Jesus rejoiced in it, and repeated it; but it was not His last word; it is not likely that He stopped short at such truth as had already been perfectly uttered by King David.

The other image of the Twenty-third Psalm is the Royal Entertainer; and this, too, recurs in the words of Jesus, but with a deepened meaning. He frequently, in His parables, compared the Gospel to a feast. Even in this world Christianity turns human life into a festival, and in the world to come the life of the blessed will be the Marriage Supper of the Lamb. For Christ brought life and immortality to light. He spoke of the world unseen as of a place native and familiar; and His own Resurrection and Ascension opened the gates of heaven to all believers. Thus what the Old Testament saints only groped after is now for us a sure possession.

Closely allied to this image is the institution of the Lord's Supper, in which Christ goes down through all the centuries, to the end of time, in the character of Royal Entertainer, with these words encircling His figure, "This Man receiveth sinners and eateth with them." Of this, Sir H. W. Baker has taken advantage in the eucharistic hymn, "The King of love my shepherd is," which is a rendering, verse by verse, of our Psalm, with only a Christian touch added

Introduction

here and there. Hardly, indeed, were even these changes necessary; for, in its naked simplicity, the Twenty-third Psalm gives such adequate expression to Christian feeling, in even its most intimate moments, that it might compete with the Hundred-and-third or the Hundred-and-sixteenth for the title of the Psalm for the Communion Table.

THE GOOD SHEPHERD

THE GOOD SHEPHERD

"The Lord is my shepherd;
I shall not want."

The handling of the material in this psalm is very artistic. The primary idea is expressed in the opening words, "The Lord is my Shepherd"; and then, to the end of v. 4, follow inferences from it, mentioning in detail the different things which one who is a good shepherd will do. Of these inferences the first is included in this first verse, "I shall not want." This is the sole negative inference; those that follow are positive.

1. A Profitable Practice.

Not long ago, on opening a new book— a translation from the Dutch—on the Lord's

B   17

The Psalm of Psalms

Parables, I was struck with the way in which the subject was divided. First were discussed the parables taken from agriculture, of which there were said to be seven ; then those taken from the work of the vinedresser, of which there were six ; then those taken from the work of the shepherd ; then those from the industry of the fisherman ; and so on.

It brought home to me more distinctly than I had ever observed before, how the common life of Palestine was all swept, for purposes of illustration, into the teaching of Christ—with what an observant and sympathetic eye He had looked upon the common occupations of men, and how suggestive they had been to Him of spiritual analogies.

I suppose, the four occupations to which I have referred were the most common in Palestine. There was, first, agriculture : this was the basis of existence, and in it the body of the people were employed. Then there was the occupation of the vinedresser : every sunny hillside was covered with vineyards, and at the time of the vintage the

The Good Shepherd

whole land was filled with the songs of those who gathered and those who trod the grapes. Then there was the occupation of the shepherd : the hills which were not suitable for the cultivation of the vine were clothed with flocks ; and every village had its droves of great and small cattle, which were led out to the pastures every evening. Then there was the labour of the fisherman, which Jesus could not possibly omit, because it was so conspicuous in the part of the country in which the principal scene of His ministry lay.

It was not only, however, nor was it first by Him that these features of common life in the Holy Land were beautifully described and used as vehicles for conveying spiritual truth. In both the poetical and prophetical parts of the Old Testament we find the same practice in full operation. How often, for example, in the Psalms and the Prophets, are the people of God compared to a vine, of which God is the husbandman ; and every single step in the history of the vineyard, from the time it is cleared of stones and fenced in from the surrounding waste on to

The Psalm of Psalms

the point where the wine is in the cup and at the owner's lips, is made use of to illustrate some aspect or other of divine truth. Still more common, if possible, is the use for the same purpose made of the shepherd's calling. As early as the age of the patriarchs, God is called the Shepherd of Israel ; and in a hundred different forms subsequently this thought recurs, every phase and incident of the life of the shepherd and the life-history of the sheep being turned to account, as in the unspeakably beautiful words of Isaiah, "He shall feed His flock like a shepherd ; He shall gather the lambs with His arm and carry them in His bosom, and shall gently lead those that are with young."

Here, then, we see a distinct and prevalent habit of the religious mind. The inspired teachers perceived in the common occupations of daily life innumerable hints and suggestions of heavenly truths, and they taught those who received their teaching to brood upon these analogies as they engaged in their ordinary occupations.

The Good Shepherd

Now this is a precious habit; and we also
—both those who teach and those who are
taught—ought to cultivate it. The aspect
of our modern life is, indeed, very different
from that ancient one. Though we still
have in our population the agriculturist, the
shepherd, and the fisherman, we are not an
agricultural but a commercial people, and we
have a vast number of other occupations.
Some of these may not be so poetical or
suggestive as the occupations of a simple
open-air existence. But many of them—
such as the calling of the builder, the banker,
the manufacturer, the engineer—are pregnant
with instructive and impressive suggestions;
and there is no occupation which is altogether
unable to yield such nutrition to the brood-
ing mind.

Existence is ennobled when, besides the
prose of mere loss and gain, its occupations
thus whisper to the heart the poetry of
spiritual suggestion; and our modern world
would be a far happier place if it had poets
who could thus interpret the hidden meaning of common things. It is not, indeed,

destitute of these ; but they are required in far greater numbers. I like to think of the poets who are still to be. There are Homers and Shakspeares, Miltons and Burnses, still to be born. The generations of the future will read glorious books which we have never seen, and be inspired with songs, full of melody and joy, which our ears have never heard. What these strains of the future will be we can only guess ; but no office of poetry is so valuable as that of dignifying common life by revealing the filaments by which it is connected with an ideal region—the life spiritual and eternal.

Meanwhile, let us be thankful for this, that every man is in some degree a poet. There is an inarticulate poetry which never goes into words or books, but warms, delights and refines the soul in which it simmers. The apprentice has it who, as he measures a yard of ribbon or sells a pound of sugar, is thinking of how trade unites the races of the world and makes all men servants one of another ; the working man has it who, as he chisels a stone for its place in a building, is thinking how the providence of daily experience is shaping himself for a place in the temple of God ; the servant has it who, as she sweeps a room or scours a vessel, is praying that her heart may be a clean abode for the habitation of God's Spirit. Even the scavenger may be rapt by it out of the gutter, where he is employed, up to the heavenly places ; and, if he is, then in the genuine attributes of manhood he far excels the gentleman in broadcloth who may despise him, as he passes, if the soul of the latter does not soar above pounds, shillings and pence.

2. A Fruitful Analogy.

Although all lawful occupations will yield some analogies to divine truth, there are, of course, certain which are more fertile in this respect than others ; and the religious language of all ages seems to prove that in the occupation of the shepherd such analogies are particularly obvious.

Perhaps, indeed, this was more the case in the East than it is in this country. The shepherds of our border hills are a superior class of men, and their care for the flocks entrusted to them is exemplary, but the Oriental shepherd was brought much nearer his sheep, and his affection for them was more peculiar. By two circumstances especially was this demonstrated—the one, the well-known fact that, instead of driving his sheep, the Oriental shepherd goes before them, whilst they follow; the other, the fact that he not only knows his own sheep by head-mark, as, I suppose, our shepherds also do, but calls each of them by its own name. In our mountains it is not unusual to see sheep on the hillside with no shepherd in sight, especially where there is an enclosing wall or fence, the presence of a shepherd being not always necessary. But in the East, sheep are never seen without the shepherd. In Eastern fields there are no fences, and danger is never far off: the wolf or the panther may be prowling about, or the robber from the desert may be on the watch. Our shepherds go out in the morning with nothing but plaid and staff; but in

The Good Shepherd

the East, even at the present day, the shepherd goes afield armed to the teeth with gun, sword, or other weapons; and it is no very unusual incident for a shepherd actually to sacrifice his life for his flock.

Of course all shepherds are not alike faithful or affectionate; but we can easily believe that David was an ideal shepherd. We remember how he slew the lion and the bear by which his flock had been attacked; and, even if we were unacquainted with these incidents, we could imagine how his generous heart would have gone out to the creatures under his charge, and how his courage would have prompted him to sacrifice himself for their protection. We may be certain of this, too, that the intensity of David's fidelity became to him an interpreter of God's faithfulness to those over whose welfare He had pledged Himself to watch. In the same way, it is the man who is himself the most affectionate and loyal father who best knows what is meant by the fatherhood of God. And in general, we may lay down the rule that it is the man who

The Psalm of Psalms

loves his occupation and is doing his daily
work with all his might who will best perceive the divine lessons it is fitted to teach.

The shepherd's care of his sheep begins
with the most elementary wants of existence,
but it mounts up, through successive stages
of attention and kindness, till it may cul-
minate in the sacrifice of his life on their
behalf. At every step this has its counter-
part in God : we are dependent on Him for
our daily bread ; and upon numerous steps
the tale of His grace has to be told, till we
come to the astounding fact that " the Good
Shepherd giveth His life for the sheep."

Thus the relation of God to the soul of
man is attractively and suggestively set forth
by the relation of the shepherd to the sheep.
Perhaps on the opposite side—the relation
of the soul to God, which is the other half of
religion—the analogy is not so serviceable.

Here also, indeed, there are pathetic hints
of the truth. The sheep has a tendency to
stray and lose itself. So all we, like sheep,
have gone astray ; we have turned every one
to his own way.

The Good Shepherd

There are some animals, such as the dog, which, though lost, have a remarkable faculty of finding their way home. The sheep is, however, I should think, deficient in this kind of intelligence: if lost, it has no instinct for finding itself again. Here also, it may be said, the analogy holds. When man lost God, he would never of his own accord have come home. God had to come after him.

But none of the righteous ever knew
　　How deep were the waters crossed,
Or how dark was the night that the Lord passed through,
　　Ere He found the sheep that was lost.
　　　　Out in the desert He heard its cry,
　　　　Sick and helpless and ready to die.

Lord, whence are those blood drops all the way
　　That mark out the mountain track?
They were shed for one who had gone astray,
　　Ere the Shepherd could bring him back.
　　　　Lord, whence are Thy hands so rent and torn?
　　　　They were pierced tonight by many a thorn.

As we say this of the human race as a whole, so of every individual soul it may be said that it never could and never would have returned of its own accord. God has to send forth His Spirit to seek, to strive and persuade. "No man can come unto Me, except the Father, which hath sent Me, draw him."

But the responsibility of man to yield to these strivings of God's Spirit, and his freedom either to continue in sin or to come home to God, are very imperfectly represented by anything in the case of the sheep. So especially is the choice by which we turn away from all other masters and acknowledge God as our own God—the most important moment of religion on man's side.

There are also other points at which the relation of the sheep to the shepherd does not express very well the relation of the soul to God. But of nearly all analogies the same is true—they illustrate only a limited number of points, while at other points they break down. And our wisdom is to bring into the light those aspects of the truth which an image fairly illustrates, letting the others fall into the background. The image of the shepherd and the sheep illustrates so many points so well that there is no need of forcing it to do work for which it was not intended.

3. A Golden Promise.

The first inference drawn from the great statement "The Lord is my shepherd," is, "I shall not want." This is merely negative; yet how priceless it is! In the strength of such a promise a pilgrim might almost travel the whole way.

Many people are haunted all their days with the fear of want; and, although they have no real trouble today, they are continually borrowing it from tomorrow, and so allowing their entire existence to be overshadowed. Many even of the young are haunted with the dread that, however well they may live and however honestly they may work, the world may have no room for them and may not even afford them their daily bread. But this is a morbid and unbelieving state of mind, and not in accordance with facts. Society is always in need of upright men and women and honest workers, and does not grudge them their wages. The fact that we have been brought into existence is a proof that we are needed ; and the likelihood is strong that a sufficient share of what is required to sustain existence will be ours, if we are willing to do our part to deserve our place. This is the cheerful philosophy of Jesus Himself: "Consider the lilies of the field how they grow : they toil not neither do they spin ; and yet I say unto you that Solomon in all his glory was not arrayed like one of these. Wherefore, if God so clothe the grass of the field, which today is, and tomorrow is cast into the oven, shall He not much more clothe you, O ye of little faith? Behold the fowls of the air: for they sow not, neither do they reap, nor gather into barns ; yet your Heavenly Father feedeth them. Are ye not much better than they?"

Can we say, then, that poverty never can overtake the godly? I once heard the late Mr. Spurgeon, in his own church, read a psalm in which this verse occurs: "I have been young and now am old, yet have I not seen the righteous forsaken, or his seed begging bread." After reading the verse, he paused and remarked, " David, being a king, may never have seen this spectacle ; but I, being a minister and better acquainted with poor people, have seen it often." That was a very bold statement. Let me quote to you another of an opposite tenor. I was once walking through a poorhouse with the manager, a wise and kindly man, and, being pained with what I had seen, I said to him, " Tell me, now, what proportion of the inmates of this house have been well-doing people, and have been brought here by no fault of their own." " Well," he answered, " I know them all well, and I am acquainted with their histories, and, I am sorry to say, there is not a single one of the sort you have indicated."

These are widely discrepant statements, and perhaps both of them might mislead. An enormous quantity of abject poverty— probably a far larger proportion of it than in the present temper of the public mind would be readily believed—is due to vice ; in our

own society it is especially due to drunkenness. Character and well-doing, on the
contrary, usually lift at least to the level of
honest poverty, with which the dignity and
sunshine of life are not incompatible. Besides, where character and well-doing are,
there is the power to rally against misfortune : poverty may crush for a time, but
the God-fearing spirit will rise above it, and
life will improve as it proceeds. On the
other hand, however, modern society is so
complex that many have to suffer for the
wrong-doing of others; and it would be
blind and cruel to doubt that sometimes the
deserving may sink into destitution, and
that in the almshouse, and even the poorhouse, there are saints of God.

What do these exceptional cases prove?
Do they prove that sometimes God's
promise fails? If we look to Jesus, we
shall understand the mystery. Though He
spoke so cheerfully of God's good providence, yet He had to say Himself, "Foxes
have holes, and the birds of the air have
nests; but the Son of man hath not where

The Good Shepherd

to lay His head"; and He died forsaken and outcast. Still, through all, He kept His eye fixed on God and never doubted that out of the darkest misfortune He would cause to be born a higher good. Nor was He disappointed; for out of His bitter shame has come His exaltation, and out of His loss and suffering the salvation of the world. So out of the mysteries of God's providence will there be born glorious surprises for His other children also. His resources are not exhausted in this life: even after death He can still justify Himself. If God causes any of His saints to want one thing, it is only that He may give a better.

> Deep in unfathomable mines
>   Of never-failing skill
> He treasures up His bright designs
>   And works His sovereign will.
>
> Ye fearful saints, fresh courage take,
>   The clouds ye so much dread
> Are big with mercy and will break
>   In blessing on your head.

REST

35

REST

"He maketh me to lie down in green pastures;
He leadeth me beside the still waters."

After, in verse 1, announcing the theme of
the Psalm to be a comparison between the
Lord's care of His people and a shepherd's
care of his flock, the sacred poet goes on to
illustrate the different kinds of fortune
through which human beings pass and in
which they experience the divine care and
sympathy; and each of these is illustrated
by a corresponding situation in the history
of the sheep under the shepherd's guidance.
Life is full of transitions and vicissitudes;
sometimes it is in sunshine, sometimes in
shadow; sometimes it is on the heights,
sometimes in the depths; but in every one

of its varying phases God is still at hand, watching over His own and doing all things well.

The imperial singer begins with prosperity, of which he gives this picture taken from the pastoral life : " He maketh me lie down in green pastures ; He leadeth me beside the still waters." This is, as someone has said, the most complete picture of happiness that ever was or can be drawn.

But why does he begin with this? Why does he describe the experience of prosperity before that of adversity? Someone has answered, Because it is the commoner state. The lot of God's people is, on the whole, one of happiness. Seasons of suffering there are, indeed ; and they are vividly remembered—just as an obstruction in a river makes a great show and causes a great noise ; but the life of the Christian is for the most part like a tranquil stream, which flows deep and does not invite attention.

Lord Bacon has the aphorism that, while prosperity was the promise of the Old Testament, adversity is the blessing of the New.

Rest

But is this true?   There are doubtless many
weighty words of the New Testament which
speak of the cross which Christians must
bear and the persecutions they may have
to suffer: "Whosoever doth not bear his
cross and come after Me, cannot be My
disciple"; "Marvel not if the world hateth
you; ye know that it hated Me before it
hated you."   Such words abound among the
sayings of our Lord and His apostles.   But
they do not stand alone; and, when quoted
alone, they convey a misleading impression.
What said the Master Himself?   "Verily,
I say unto you, there is no man who hath
left house, or brethren or sisters, or father
or mother, or wife or children, for My sake
and the gospel's, but he shall receive a
hundredfold more in this time, houses, and
brethren and sisters, and mothers and children, and lands, with persecutions; and in
the world to come eternal life."   Similarly
an apostle declares: "Godliness is profitable
unto all things, having promise of the life
which now is and of that which is to come."
The New Testament is not a sadder book

than the Old; on the contrary, it is far more sunny and melodious; and this is not only because the misery of the present life is to be compensated by the felicity of the life to come, but this life itself is a happy one.

> The world's no blank to us
> Nor blot; it means intensely, and means good.

I. TEMPORAL PROSPERITY.

This is true in regard to temporal prosperity. The tendency of things is to throw into the lap of God's people the best blessings even of this earthly life.

What are these? Health is one of them. This is a fundamental blessing, on which many more depend. All sights look dreary when seen through the jaundiced eyes of disease, and all pleasures are tasteless when they touch an unhealthy palate. But, when the blood is flowing limpidly through the veins and the brain is fresh and unclogged, God's glorious world, with its sights and sounds, gratifies the senses and awakens desire; things have their natural taste, and the simple elements of life are enough to satisfy without the condiment of artificial pleasure. Now, health is most likely to be the heritage of those who obey the laws of God. By the excesses of an ungoverned youth, many are sowing in their own bodily constitution the seeds of a debilitated manhood and an early death. They are burning out in themselves the very sense for natural pleasure and creating the necessity for artificial stimulation, which loses its effect the oftener it is applied. Those who listen to the voice of God and follow the path of virtue may be scoffed at, because, during the opportunities of youth, they do not follow the hot and highly seasoned pleasures which others pursue; but their enjoyment lasts longer, and at the period when others are falling bankrupt they are coming into the full enjoyment of their heritage.

Another of the best blessings of life is love. It is by the heart mainly that human beings are made blessed or miserable; and it is a notable evidence of the equality of nature that love is restricted to no class or grade of culture or fortune. The poorest may feel the glow of pure affection and be loyal to the vows of friendship. Love culminates in the home, and he who possesses a happy home, where the hunger of the heart is satisfied and the voice of innocent mirth is heard, has not missed the best which this earthly life can yield. But to whom does the blessing of love belong? Many prostitute the name by applying it to indulgences which make true love impossible ; for impurity " hardens a' within and petrifies the feeling." He who wastes his youth is robbing himself beforehand of the power of giving to a pure woman, should he be so fortunate as to win the love of such a one, heart for heart ; he is robbing himself beforehand of the power of looking in his children's faces unashamed ; and it is more than possible that his offspring may have to pay with lives of misery the penalty of his sin. If the glory of friendship is that each friend knows the other to be absolutely transparent and true ; if love is the exchange of hearts which have been kept for one another unspent and undefiled ; if home is, as has been said, the one bit of Paradise left in a fallen world ; then is the gift of love, in all its perfection and splendour, peculiarly the heritage of those who have taken God's law and Christ's will as the rule of their life.

Another of these blessings is business success. Of this, indeed, too high an estimate may be formed. In a business community financial success is deified, and multitudes, though perhaps they are hardly aware of the fact, worship no other God. On the other hand, it is possible to depreciate success too much. Business is, by the allotment of Providence, that to which the majority have to devote the most of their time and the best of their strength. To depreciate it, therefore, as if it did not matter whether or not a man did it with all his might, is only to confuse the mind and perplex the conscience. Business is a providential school of virtue, in which manhood is developed and the natural powers are exercised, and success is, as a rule, the evidence that we have not been faithless or laggard scholars. To whom does success fall? Some would answer, To the selfish and unscrupulous — to those who mind Number One and never hesitate to fling down or trample on a competitor, and to those who, when occasion requires, can, without flinching, stoop to falsehood. Alas, there are too many facts which might be adduced in support of such a view of business. Yet it is a partial view, and there is a vast body of facts on the opposite side. Unscrupulousness sometimes succeeds, and often quite eclipses honesty in the rapidity with which it reaches the goal ; but its prosperity is frequently short-lived and its hollowness is exposed at last. Character tells in business. It may not do so today, but it will tomorrow. "The meek," said our Lord, "shall inherit the earth." It seems a paradox ; for are not the meek thrust aside and trampled in an age like ours by the pushing and self-assertive? Yes, they are ; but their turn comes. The gilt of pretentious talents is soon rubbed off, and then what it has covered looks shabby ; but the

Rest

solid gold of character shines more and more the longer it is rubbed, and in due time its value is acknowledged. There are those who will tell you that the Decalogue is abrogated in the business-world, and that the Sermon on the Mount, though beautiful to read in a castle-in-the-air, has no meaning in the market-place. But the Decalogue and the Sermon on the Mount have a way of living on, whilst their critics pass away. Some men also venture to take these rules into the market-place; and the God who made the Decalogue and the Christ who preached the Sermon do not allow them to be put to shame.

Some possess all these blessings of the earthly life which I have mentioned and many more besides. They have the gift of health; they have known love in all its sweet, pure forms; their friends are warm and true; their home is a scene of tranquillity in which they find refuge from the turmoils of the world; their children are affectionate and well-doing; and God has so blessed the labour of their hands that they have never lacked bread to eat or raiment to put on.

The Psalm of Psalms

The lines have fallen unto them in pleasant places. Theirs is the condition our text describes : "He maketh me to lie down in green pastures ; He leadeth me beside the still waters."

God has given these gifts. With what effect on the relation between your soul and Him ? It is an astonishing thing how often in Scripture spiritual improvement is ascribed to affliction and misfortune. "Before I was afflicted I went astray, but now I have learned thy law." "Whom the Lord loveth He chasteneth, and scourgeth every son whom He receiveth." In experience, too, we find that religious improvement is closely connected with suffering. Hundreds of times we have heard of sinners being converted by a severe illness or a great bereavement ; but who ever heard of a man being converted by a windfall of good fortune ? It is not creditable that we are thus dependent for our religion on the withdrawal of temporal blessings and so little affected by the possession of them.

I do not, however, believe that loss alone

sanctifies. Happiness does so too. A heart made happy by pure love is not far from the kingdom of God. The coming of a child into a family sometimes opens the door for Christ. Prosperity in business breeds liberality in giving. Only, such virtues ought far oftener to spring from God's goodness. Many of us, if we would only, in a sequestered hour, look back on the way we have been led, and look round on the ample and sunny heritage in which God has placed us, could see a thousand reasons for clinging with boundless gratitude and loyalty to Him and to the kingdom of His Son.

2. SPIRITUAL PROSPERITY.

When, however, the psalmist says, "Thou makest me to lie down in green pastures, Thou leadest me beside the still waters," he cannot be referring to temporal blessings alone: this is also a description of the life spiritual.

Valuable as temporal blessings are, a Christian must hold them with a light hand

and be ready to sacrifice them for the sake of the integrity of the life within. Christians have, in fact, often thus sacrificed every worldly possession and every worldly prospect and laid down even life itself. A Christian lives in the world like other men ; he attends to business and derives profits from it ; he enjoys the delight of friendship and the comfort of home ; yet he has, at the same time, a life which ordinary men of the world have not—a life remote and solitary, hid with Christ in God. A portion of human nature which in other men is dormant has in him been awakened ; he is in living intercourse with the world unseen ; the powers of his spirit are in activity, going forth towards their proper objects—to God, to Christ, to truth, to eternity.

Now this spiritual life, taken as a whole, is a supremely happy life, and brings fresh currents of joy into the being. So voluminous are these that they are able to make up for the loss of ordinary temporal comforts and enjoyments. Look at a man like St. Paul. He lost much by being a Christian ;

he suffered much; but was he an unhappy man? On the contrary, an exuberant life throbs in all his movements, and an irrepressible joy rings, like a peal of bells, in all his writings.

What are the enjoyments of this hidden life?

One of them is love. I have already spoken of the deep pleasure of ordinary human love. But the heart of man has been fashioned with the capacity for a love profounder and nobler than the love of friend or father, wife or child. We are capable of loving God and His Son Jesus Christ. In many hearts this is a capacity and nothing more, just as other forms of affection may never reach their realisation. Many do not love God; they do not love the Saviour. But where this divine affection is awakened into activity, it is not only the most sacred and influential, but also the most delightful and satisfying emotion which the heart can know. If to love another human being, and to know that you are held dear by another human heart, be one of the crowning experiences of life, what must it be to love God and to know that you are held dear in the heart of Christ?

It is almost choosing at random from a wide field of selection, when I mention as another of the enjoyments of the interior life delight in the Word of God. I mention this because the words of our text have often been applied to it. When enjoying revealed truth, Christians often speak of themselves as lying down in green pastures and being led beside still waters. Thus one says, "What are these green pastures but the Scriptures of truth—always fresh, always rich, and never exhausted? Sweet and full are the doctrines of the gospel, fit food for souls, as tender grass is nutriment for sheep. When by faith we are enabled to find rest in the promises, we are like the sheep that lie down in the midst of pastures ; we find at the same moment both provender and peace, rest and refreshment, serenity and satisfaction." There are those who read the Bible and enjoy it for its literary qualities alone ; and, indeed, by its profundity of thought and beauty of diction, it is placed at the head of all literature. But the delight of a spiritual mind in it is deeper : the Bible is one of the principal means through which it maintains its connexion and intercourse with the divine heart which it loves.

Let me name but one more enjoyment of the hidden life—the bliss of doing good. This bliss is not, indeed, the exclusive property of the spiritual. There are those who, from natural goodness of heart or the influence of good tradition and training, care continually for the welfare of their neighbours ; and none can do so, whatever be their motives, without having a rich blessing returned into their own bosoms. But the passion of doing good belongs peculiarly to Christians. They have learned it from Christ. Looking on their fellow-men through His eyes, they perceive both their infinite worth and their immeasurable danger. Having received salvation themselves, they feel an instinctive desire to communicate the secret to others. In this work many emotions are stirred, some of them painful and some pleasurable. It is work which is liable to encounter opposition; and the opposition may wax deadly. But, on the whole, the reward of such work is great. No man ever yet exerted himself for the temporal and eternal welfare of others without being himself enriched. And, when the work is successful, and men and women are saved, and they pour their gratitude on our heads, who can measure the joy? It is worth living for, to be made the instrumentality through which has been wrought an immortal good.

This is what some would call, not without a touch of contempt, the hedonistic or eudæmonistic aspect of Christianity; and they would deprecate the emphasizing of this pleasurable element in religion. Better, they would say, emphasize the sober fact that religion is a duty to be done, a yoke to be felt, a cross to bear. I do not, however, think so. Let each side of the truth have its turn. And, after all, Christianity must always be far more a gift from God to man than a gift from man to God.

Rest

It is of the utmost consequence to proclaim and reiterate that the blessedness of man is hidden at the centre of his own being : it lies in the opening up of the hidden world of the spirit, into which Christianity invites him. It is there that man meets God and enters into the fulness of salvation by Jesus Christ. Let no one leave the world without seeing the one vision it contains, or die without ever having lived.

DISCIPLINE

DISCIPLINE

Verse Third.

"He restoreth my soul;
He leadeth me in the paths of righteousness for His
name's sake."

In the Twenty-third Psalm the different kinds
of experience through which the people of
God pass are set forth by different incidents
in the life of a flock of sheep. The point
is, that the shepherd is always present and
watchful, consulting for the welfare of the
creatures committed to his care; and in the
same way God is with His people in every
variety of fortune, seeing to it that all things
work together for their good. Verse 2 is a
perfect picture of prosperity; but verse 3 is
a picture of adversity.

The Psalm of Psalms

1. THE FAINTING-FITS OF THE SOUL.

"He restoreth my soul," says the sacred singer. But this implies that the soul is in need of restoration. The picture is that of a sheep which, through heat and fatigue, has fainted away, or is on the point of breathing out its life; but the good shepherd, by administering a restorative in the nick of time, brings back the departing breath. Here we have a totally different picture from that of verse 2. There the sheep was in green pastures; all was sunshine and happiness; life was enjoyable and abundant. But here life is at the lowest ebb; and the sheep has fainted away.

There are such contrasts in experience. Life has its sunshine, but it has also its shadow. There are days of prosperity, when the tides swell the channel of life from bank to brae; but there are also times of adversity, when the pulse of life is low and hope has almost died out of the heart.

This is the case even in the Christian life. On the whole, it is a life of joy—it is the

Discipline

happiest of all lives—yet it has its seasons of faintness and despair, when the cordials and restoratives of the Good Shepherd are required.

What are the reasons for these fainting times ?

First of all, a Christian is exposed, like other men, to the misfortunes and calamities of the human lot. There is a passage of Scripture which says that God maketh His sun to rise on the evil and on the good, and sendeth His rain on the just and unjust : there are certain common blessings in which all participate, whatever be their character. But the converse is also true, that there are common misfortunes from which none escape, be their character what it may. The lightning strikes the roof of sinner and saint indiscriminately ; a bad harvest destroys the crops of good and bad alike ; bad times blight the business of the honest as well as of the dishonest ; illness and death are incident to all the children of men. At many points, indeed, godliness will supply alleviations of even such common calamities : when an epidemic is raging, the steady man's chances of recovery are much greater than those of him who has wasted his constitution by dissipation; and, in times when trade fails, the industrious and saving have generally something to fall back on, whereas the reckless, who live from hand to mouth, are thrown on the rocks at once. Still there is in this world a mysterious body of evil from which none can altogether escape. "Man is born to trouble as the sparks fly upwards," and, the more complicated life becomes, through the crowding of population, the more is the individual exposed to suffering for which he is not directly responsible.

Further, however, Christians are exposed to suffering through the very fact that they are Christians. Christ had to warn His first followers that they would be hated of all men for His sake. "Yea, the time cometh," He said, "when whosoever killeth you will think he doeth God service." In many ages this has been literally fulfilled, as is proved by the religious persecutions of ancient and modern times. Nor has the offence of the

Discipline

cross ever ceased. Public persecution has, indeed, ceased, but private persecution still continues; and it is sometimes harder to bear. The natural heart is still unchanged; and it resents the disturbance to its self-complacency caused by the presence and the criticism of the followers of Jesus. In the archives of the Church we have our books of martyrs, and these are by no means all written yet; but the unwritten persecutions are infinitely vaster in their proportions, and they form one of the causes from which the flock of God faints.

There are, however, deeper causes still. The Christian life has its own special pains and secret crosses. A Christian is a man who has seen an ideal: Christ is his ideal, and the life of Christ is the model with which he is always comparing his own. This breeds a divine discontent; he despises himself; he is often in despair because he has fallen beneath what he ought to be. Perhaps he has been on the heights of communion, inspiration and holiness; but the tides of the Spirit recede, the heart grows cold, indifference comes on, iniquity prevails against him. Even a St. Paul had to cry out in bitterness of spirit, " Oh, wretched man that I am, who shall deliver me from the body of this death ? "

To mention but one other cause of the fainting-fits of the soul : Christians have on their shoulders and on their hearts the public cause of Christ, and, when it is in difficulties or is threatened with failure, they have to bear the burden and the shame. Sometimes it seems as if at the back of Christianity there were no almighty force ; the world is too strong for it ; ancient forms of wrong cannot be overcome ; and wickedness, enthroned in high places, is scornful and insolent. In such cases the ungodly are always ready to exult and ask, " Where is your God now gone ? " The Christian may feel in his own heart that his prayers are not being answered ; perhaps someone near and dear to him is under the power of a vice from which even religion seems unable to deliver him ; and the heart faints with the strain of unceasing shame and long delay.

Discipline

I have described the occasions of depression
at length; but the Psalm does not do so.
What it says is not, " I have many causes of
trouble," but, " He restoreth my soul." It
is as if the only element of the time of suffering which was remembered was the deliverance
from it.

Man's extremity is God's opportunity.
The sympathy, the tenderness, and the loving
kindness of God would not be fully known
were it not for the days of darkness in which
He draws near to succour.

If God is ever certain to be near His saints,
it is when they are in trouble. Which of all
the sheep in a good shepherd's flock is the
most certain to have the shepherd's attention?
Is it not the one that is ailing? As soon as
the cry of distress is heard from afar, see how
the shepherd hastens over flood and scaur,
leaving the ninety-and-nine to look after
themselves. Of a mother's children, which
is the one that receives most assiduity? Is

63

it not the one that is in danger? When a child is laid down with fever or has had an accident, the mother's thoughts are never for a moment out of the room; the love in her heart increases with the danger, till it becomes painful in its intensity, and she takes no rest till the life is restored. Such human experiences make us acquainted with the heart of God; for the sparks of affection in our composition have been kindled from the fire of love in His nature. Never is He so near, never is His compassion so melting, as when we need Him most. And, when this is realised, the storm within us is changed into a calm. Any grief is bearable if we are able to say, My Shepherd knows.

But what are the restoratives with which God overcomes the fainting-fits of those who put their trust in Him?

They are numerous, and it would be impossible to specify them all. Sometimes, when adversity has lasted long, He causes it to be followed by a time of prosperity; and the joy of His goodness is all the greater because of the contrast with preceding suffer-

Discipline

ing. The night may be dark, but the day succeeds the night; the rain may be continuous, and the storm may roar as if it would sweep man with all his works off the face of the earth, but the sunshine succeeds the rain, and calm comes after the storm. In the times of persecution which our forefathers had to endure, being hunted like partridges on the mountains, there came now and then, owing to various causes, longer or shorter periods when the zeal of the persecutor slackened and the persecuted were allowed repose. These pauses were called "blinks," and they were greatly enjoyed. At such times their souls were restored. Even in the lives which are most sorely beset with misfortune there are "blinks"; God knows that the human spirit is not able to bear the unceasing strain of calamity, and He gives these intervals of rest. When one source of comfort or joy is taken away, the vacant place is filled with a new one. Thus, into a home from which someone greatly beloved has been removed there is sent a new child; the bereaved hearts revive to welcome the young life; and the cypresses of the grave are hidden beneath the climbing roses of hope.

Sometimes it turns out that the road of adversity is the pathway to prosperity, and apparent calamity is only the disguise in which good fortune is for a little concealed. One of the most famous men of our century has put it on record that what appeared the misfortunes of his early life turned out in the end to be the steps to influence and renown. Again and again he attempted to find refuge from the stress of circumstances by putting into some little haven of commonplace comfort, where he might have lived and died a nonentity; but Providence shut up the way in every case and kept him out on the high seas, where, by battling with the storms, he acquired courage and power, and in due time he came to his kingdom. Providence seems sometimes to delight in steering the course of its favourites to the very verge of ruin, till the heart of the voyager quakes with terror, when suddenly, by a skilful turn of the Pilot's hand, the vessel is guided

Discipline

into the sunny seas of undreamed-of success ; and the poor human heart, which was half-dead with dismay, is filled with laughter and the tongue with song. If in the spiritual world there are seasons of dryness and of decline, when the tree of life appears to wither, there are also times of revival, when the breath of spring is in the atmosphere and the movement of spring in the ground —the flowers appear on the earth, the time of the singing of birds is come, and the voice of the turtle is heard in the land. Over a congregation, or a city, or a country, there passes the wind of the Spirit of God ; religion suddenly becomes real ; the powers of the world to come can almost be seen and handled ; and to be alive is a joy. This may be brought about for the individual through slight means—by meeting with a new friend, by the influence of a good minister, by a little success in winning souls, by realising some new truth of God's Word, or the like. The Christian life is a succession of new beginnings; and they that wait on the Lord shall renew their strength.

The Psalm of Psalms

3. THE BEST USE OF ADVERSITY.

The Psalm directs special attention to one of the uses of adversity in the words, "He leadeth me in the paths of righteousness."

Here the poet is holding fast by his metaphor ; because it is a fact that in times of peril and fear the sheep of a flock follow close to the shepherd, and keep in a straight path wherever he may lead them. At other times they can expatiate over the fields and may easily wander ; but terror makes them keep their eye on the shepherd and follow him without turning to the right hand or the left.

But how true to human experience also is the statement ! Adversity has a great deal to do with sanctification.

For one thing, it makes prayer real. Some of us would, I daresay, confess that we never knew what prayer actually was till we were driven to the throne of grace by a calamity that was brea ing our heart. I remember being in Germany immediately after the Franco-Prussian War ; and I was told how, during the anxious months of the

Discipline

war-time, the churches, which usually are so empty in that country, were crowded, every time the doors were opened, with fathers and mothers whose sons were at the front. Prayer in days which are without suffering or change is apt to be only a pious form, of which we are weary ; but, when the heart is dreading some impending calamity or the iron of loss has entered into the soul, the old forms are filled with fresh meaning, and the tides of emotion overflow the forms ; we do not measure the time which we spend on our knees, and the words of prayer pour, new and living, from the heart.

The same might be said of the Bible : we read it with opened eyes when we have suffered. Passages which we have read scores of times without seeing their beauty lay hold of our sympathy. Deep calls unto deep—the experience of the writer finds its echo in our breasts. What Goethe said of poetry is true of Scripture :

> Who never ate his bread in sorrow,
>   Who never spent the midnight hours
> Weeping and watching for the morrow,
>   He knows you not, ye heavenly powers.

The Psalm of Psalms

Thus by the avenue of prayer and by the avenue of the Word we are brought nigh to God through adversity ; but adversity affects character in many other ways. I have known a Christian who, after years of careful living and useful testimony, fell into a state of carelessness and backsliding. Just at this stage a younger brother of his own came from the country to the city, and took up his abode in the same lodging. The younger had expected to receive from the elder a good example ; but, not receiving it, he fell into evil courses, and the issue was disastrous in the extreme. But it terrified the backsliding brother back to his Lord. Thus are we sometimes taught, by the consequences of backsliding in ourselves or others, how evil and how bitter a thing it is to depart from the living God ; and the immovable firmness with which a man stands in the right path, avoiding the very appearance of evil, may be due to the recollection of a fall and its calamitous consequences.

But, in whatever way adversity may lead us in the paths of righteousness and away from the paths of unrighteousness, this is by far the most blessed effect it can produce ; for to a Christian nothing is so good as holiness and nothing so formidable as sin. We all naturally desire prosperity and seek to avoid adversity ; but well may we say, Welcome adversity, welcome suffering, welcome the chastisements of God, if by these we are led in the paths of righteousness.

4. The Best Guarantee of Prosperity.

The phrase with which this verse closes is not to be neglected—the phrase, " for His name's sake "—because, though the wording of it is brief, the meaning is profound.

Surely God restores the souls of His sheep and leads them in the paths of righteousness for their sakes. When we are in distress, He pities us ; and pity causes Him to give aid. So, when He is leading us in the paths of righteousness, He is doing us a great kindness ; for there is nothing either so discreditable or so miserable to a child of

The Psalm of Psalms

God as to be walking in the path of unrighteousness. But the Psalm takes a far
bolder line : it says that God must do these
things for His own sake.

If we look again at the image of the shepherd, we easily see how just this observation
is. A shepherd succours his sheep when
they are fainting, and leads them back into
the straight path when they have gone astray,
for their sake—because he is attached to
them—but is not his own character involved
in the matter ? Would not the countryside
ring with his dishonour if in such circumstances he neglected his sheep and left them
to die ? So the honour of God is involved
in the welfare of His people. He has
undertaken their salvation; and, having
begun the good work, He must complete
it. If God's people were uniformly unfortunate, the young and the timid would
be terrified away from religion. It brings
reproach on the name of God when His
professing people become backsliders.

This is a strong argument to use in
prayer : we can ask Him to save us from

our sins and to make us holy, because nothing reflects such credit on His cause as the consistency of those who have named the name of Christ. Nothing can give us stronger hope in praying for friends or relatives who may have fallen under the power of sin : " Good Shepherd, lead them back to the paths of righteousness for Thine own name's sake." Such a form of prayer will impart dignity also to our own lives. We are too apt to seek deliverance from adversity for our own sakes alone ; we wish to be in the sunshine of prosperity simply because it is more pleasant to ourselves. But life ought to have a nobler aim. God's glory ought to be our chief end ; and, if man is earnestly seeking to glorify God, God will see to it that he also enjoys Him forever.

IN EXTREMIS

IN EXTREMIS

"Yea, though I walk through the valley of the shadow
of death,
I will fear no evil; for Thou art with me:
Thy rod and Thy staff, they comfort me."

THERE is some difficulty about the correct
translation of this verse. In ancient Hebrew
manuscripts there were no vowels; only the
consonants are written, the vowels having to
be supplied by the reader. This sometimes
introduces considerable uncertainty. And in
the present case it depends on the vowel or
vowels supplied by the reader whether the
rendering shall be "the valley of shadows"
or "the valley of the shadow of death."
The latter phrase, even if it be incorrect, is
in some respects an extremely happy one,
and it has obtained so strong a hold in every-

77

The Psalm of Psalms

day speech that it is neither likely nor desirable that it should be displaced. Yet I am inclined to think that "the valley of shadows" is what the writer intended to say.

It reminds us of a phrase in another famous Psalm, "the valley of Baca," which probably means "Weeping." So the Revised Version renders it :

Passing through the Valley of Weeping, they make it
    a place of springs;
Yea, the early rain covereth it with blessings.

"The valley of shadows" and "the valley of weeping" must have the same meaning. They are expressions for a particularly trying portion of that ideal journey which all must travel between the cradle and the grave.

It is more than possible, however, that there may have been some actual place bearing the name of the Valley of Shadows in the scenery from which the imagery of this Psalm is borrowed. Somewhere in the hills of Judah, where David kept his flocks, there was a glen through which, at nightfall, the shepherd boy used to lead home his sheep. They called it the Valley of Shadows or the Valley of the Shadow of Death; because there the darkness fell earlier than elsewhere, and the gloom of night was deeper. Its ravines were haunted by wild beasts; and, as the darkness came on, the distant howl of wolf or hyæna could be heard. David could remember how, at such moments, his sheep huddled closely about his heels, and he prepared to do battle, if necessary, for their lives. Since then he had learned that the life of man has also such passages; but, as the sheep crept under his protection, so he had learned where to place his trust: "Yea, though I walk through the valley of the shadow of death, I will fear no evil; for Thou art with me: Thy rod and Thy staff, they comfort me."

1. The Dark Valley.

The chief objection to the translation, "the valley of the shadow of death," is that it tends to make us think too exclusively of death as the portion of experience here intended. The dark valley may, however, occur at other stages of the journey of life.

It will be remembered where, in the *Pilgrim's Progress*, the Valley of the Shadow of Death comes in. It is not at the end, but in the first half of the pilgrim's journey. In thus locating it Bunyan was taking a justifiable liberty, guided by his personal experience; and never has the scene itself been more graphically described. You remember that perilous path, with a ditch on one side and a quagmire on the other, so that, "when the pilgrim sought to shun the ditch on the one hand, he was ready to tip over into the mire on the other; also, when he sought to escape the mire, without great carefulness he would be ready to fall into the ditch." The Valley was dark as pitch, and full of hobgoblins, satyrs and dragons of the pit; "also he heard doleful voices and rushings to and fro"; and the path was beset with snares and nets, holes and pitfalls. Under this imagery Bunyan bodies forth the spiritual conflicts and terrors, amounting almost to melancholy madness, with which the earlier stages of his own Christian course were beset, and of which such graphic and moving descriptions are found in his autobiography, *Grace Abounding*. These terrible sufferings were, in large measure, due to a nervous temperament. The elements of his nature were dangerously poised ; as was the case in a still more extreme degree with another great Englishman of Christian genius—the poet Cowper. But there are many who, if asked to say what to them had been the valley of the shadow of death, would at once think of the period when they were passing through the conviction of sin, so keen was the pain and so deadly the despair which they then endured.

In the case of others, whose temperament is not so highly strung, the causes are more realistic. While there are some lives which move on equably from beginning to end with the smoothness of a boat on a canal, in most there is considerable vicissitude of joy and sorrow, as in the course of a ship which sails the high seas and has to encounter all kinds of weather ; and in most also there occur, at least once or twice, crises and catastrophes, when feeling is put on the utmost strain, and the vital forces seem on the point of being crushed out by overwhelming pressure from without or within. We speak of experiences which can turn a person's hair grey, or out of which people emerge as if they had risen from their graves. It is to such extraordinary crises that the description of the text applies.

They may be due to a thousand different causes. Some of these may be public. A great war, for example, may put an enormous strain on the feelings of the inhabitants of a country : when, for weeks and months, tens of thousands of hearts are on the rack for the news of victory or defeat, and every list of killed and wounded that appears is scanned in feverish terror of seeing the name of husband, son or brother. The passage of a devastating epidemic through a city may have a similar effect : when at every turn in the streets the passing hearse is met, and for months the wings of death seem to be flapping about every house. Sometimes a commercial panic works in the same way: when a great bank shuts its door, whereupon failure follows failure, the gentlewoman and the widow are reduced from affluence to beggary, and no man knows but the next letter he opens may inform him that the blow has fallen on his own home.

The private causes of such sufferings are too numerous to be even hinted at. Who can estimate what a wife suffers when she first perceives that her husband is becoming a victim of drink? An honest man, with a beloved wife and a young family depending on him, who is suddenly deprived of work and sees no prospect of being able to keep the wolf from the door, must sometimes in a few weeks pass through the bitterness of death. When a heart that has trusted another and given its whole happiness into its keeping discovers at the critical moment that it has been deceived, it must appear as if the whole universe were falling and as if mankind were nothing but a lie.

But, whether the sacred poet intended it or not, it is not without significance that this experience has been called the Valley of the Shadow of Death. Death is for mankind the great Valley of Shadows. Tens of thousands would say that their bereavements had robbed them of the sap and buoyancy of life and made them old—when the mother sat by the bedside and saw the life ebbing away from the son who was the apple of her eye; when the husband laid in the grave the half of his life; when the friend lost the friend whose praise was the chief incentive to high endeavour. Death to many is an event the very thought of which simply stupefies. The stoppage of work, the interruption of plans, the forced renunciation of pleasures, the separation from the near and dear which it implies, are bewildering and horrifying; and still worse is the voyage out into the unknown, with the new experiences which may have to be encountered there. Of all enemies Death is not only the last but the worst. It was one who knew human nature well that said:

> The weariest and most loathed worldly life
> Which age, want, penury and imprisonment
> Can lay on nature is a Paradise
> To what we fear of death.

2. The Presence of God.

Again the poet is back among the experiences of his early days. As the sheep entered the Valley of the Shadows, fear huddled them close round the shepherd; but through contact with his body they became fearless; his well-known voice soothed them; even the touch of his crook, laid on them to keep them together, filled them with confidence.

It has often been asked what is the difference between the rod and the staff, but no very satisfactory answer has, as far as I am aware, been given. Some have regarded the words as two names for the same thing: but this is unlikely, as it would be a manifest tautology. Although it cannot be proved from the modern ·customs of the East, it is most probable that the ancient shepherd carried with him two instruments of his trade—one rod of lighter make, to be used in dealing with the sheep, and another of heavier weight and shod with iron, for the purpose of dealing with the enemies of

The Psalm of Psalms

the sheep, striking at the lion or the bear which might attack them. At all events, in God there are resources corresponding to both : He has all that is required for both the guidance and the protection of His own.

The peace and contentment of the sheep are not, however, due to the rod and staff, but to the bearer of them. And the secret of the heart's peace is God Himself—" I will fear no evil ; for Thou art with me." It is a universal experience that fear departs when the appropriate person is near on whose love, strength or wisdom we can rely. A child dreads to be alone in an empty house ; but to be there along with its mother makes fear impossible. A boy lost in the crowd cries as if his heart would break ; but, carried through the crowd on his father's shoulder, he is as happy as a king. As the train rushes through the night at the rate of fifty miles an hour, what a panic it would cause if the passengers should learn that no one was on the engine ; but, when they have reason to believe that the engineer is with them, they fear no evil.

In Extremis

The prisoner placed at the bar charged with a crime of which he knows himself to be innocent would be lost if left to himself to unwind the rope which the sophistical skill of the prosecutor is twisting round his neck; but, when he looks at the advocate who is with him, armed with complete knowledge of the facts and with brilliant powers of argument, he is not afraid.

There can be no circumstances in which God is not with His own. It has been pointed out that the four verses about the Good Shepherd in the Twenty-third Psalm correspond in a remarkable way with four names of God—verse 1, "The Lord is my Shepherd, I shall not want," with Jehovah-jireh, the Lord will provide; verse 2, "He maketh me to lie down in green pastures: He leadeth me beside the still waters," with Jehovah-shalom, the Lord is our peace; verse 3, "He restoreth my soul: He leadeth me in the paths of righteousness for His name's sake," with Jehovah-tsidkenu, the Lord our righteousness; and verse 4, "Yea, though I walk through the valley of the shadow of

The Psalm of Psalms

death, I will fear no evil : for Thou art with me ; Thy rod and Thy staff they comfort me," with Jehovah-shammah, the Lord is there.

Jehovah-shammah is one of the watchwords of the spiritual life. Ascend I into heaven, He is there ; descend I into hell, He is there. Be my lot in sunshine or in darkness, in health or in sickness, He is there. When I am on a bed of weakness, when I am drawing my latest breath, and when I stand before the great white throne, still Jehovah-shammah, the Lord will be there ; and I will fear no evil.

This is a secret which thousands of times has transmuted the bed of death from a place of fear and mortal defeat into a scene of victory and transfiguration. This is the secret : "Lo, I am with you alway even to the end of the world. Amen."

THE ROYAL ENTERTAINER

THE ROYAL ENTERTAINER

"Thou preparest a table before me in the presence of
    mine enemies:
Thou anointest mine head with oil;
My cup runneth over."

AT the fifth verse, it is manifest, the figure
of speech is changed. Up to this point
every clause has been a picture from the
experience of the sheep; but, when the
singer says, "Thou preparest a table before
me in the presence of mine enemies; thou
anointest mine head with oil; my cup runneth over," it is obvious that the figure of
the sheep and the shepherd is entirely
dropped.

1. THE NEW FIGURE OF SPEECH.

If at this point the figure of speech is
changed, it is a question what the next
figure is.

The Psalm of Psalms

In a published sermon, characterized by spiritual power and especially by the vividness imparted to the interpretation of the Old Testament by knowledge of the Orient, Principal George Adam Smith takes this verse as a picture of a scene from pastoral life. He thinks the speaker is a fugitive who, having committed some crime, is pursued by the avengers of blood, and has taken refuge in the tent of a shepherd-chief. By Eastern law and custom such a fugitive would be protected with all the resources of the person on whose mercy he had cast himself, and regaled with the best which the encampment could afford. It is a truly tragic picture to see the fugitive there within, protected by the sheikh and feasting on the best, while his infuriated and bloodthirsty foes glare at him from the opposite side of the threshold, which they dare not cross. Principal Smith takes these pursuing enemies to represent the writer's sins. The spectres of guilt pursue every son of man, for who has not behind him an evil past? But, if a man has taken refuge in God, casting himself on His mercy, his pursuers dare not touch him. Undoubtedly this gives a striking sense to the verse; and the interpretation has this recommendation, that it still adheres to the pastoral life. But the author is not so happy in explaining the sixth verse.

By the perusal of a fascinating booklet, entitled *The Song of our Syrian Guest*, from the pen of the Rev. W. A. Knight, the minds of multitudes on both sides of the Atlantic have been captured for the view that the image of shepherd and sheep is continued to the end of the Psalm. For the fifth verse this is argued ingeniously, but not convincingly: the preparing of a table being taken as the selection of a pasture, the anointing as the salving of wounds and bruises, and the cup as the vessel by which the trough is filled out of which the sheep drink. Far more natural is the application of the language to the various features of a banquet. But it is in the sixth verse that that interpretation breaks down. A sheep does not dwell in the "house" of a shep-

The Psalm of Psalms

herd, unless it be a pet lamb; and this is a condition which does not last "forever." No doubt the word "house" has great latitude of application; and it might possibly refer to the fold, though I do not remember a case where it is so used. When "the house of the Lord" is taken as the palace of the king, in which the banquet of the fifth verse has taken place, the sixth verse is the climax of the whole Psalm, as from its position it ought to be; but under any other interpretation this character is lost.

In short, David is here making use of the experience of the second portion of his own life, as in the image of the shepherd and the sheep he utilises the experience of the first. As in youth he was a shepherd abiding in the fields, in manhood he was a king living in a palace. One of the obligations of a king is to be an entertainer, exercising a frequent and a splendid hospitality. In this virtue, we know from the historical records of his reign, David did not come short; he had the cordiality and the personal fascination by which hospitality is rendered delightful. Many a guest had he made happy at his table, thereby binding him in triple loyalty to his own person ; and, as in his own conduct as a shepherd he had found a fruitful image of what God had done, so does he find in this other *rôle*, played by himself with such distinction, an ampler and more intimate representation of the divine goodness.

2. An Image of Activity.

Why is it that the sacred singer forsakes the image of the shepherd and the sheep, and embraces in his poem this one also? I have already given an external reason in the two periods of David's history ; but there is an internal reason as well : it is that the first image is not sufficient to express the spiritual life in its entirety. Some aspects of it were expressed by this image admirably, but others, no less important, could hardly be expressed at all.

For example, it expressed the passive but not the active side of religion.

The Psalm of Psalms

The relation of the sheep to the shepherd is wholly passive : the sheep is fed, it is led, it is protected ; a sheep does nothing for itself, or next to nothing. And there is a side of religion which corresponds to this : in religion God does everything, and man has nothing to do but passively receive. This is a great truth ; but it is not the whole truth. Religion has an active side as well : it is a battle and a victory. Well was David aware of this : he was a great worker for God, a fighter and a victor ; and this side of his religion is expressed in this next image.

Perhaps this is most distinctly hinted at in the phrase, "in the presence of mine enemies," because this denotes that it is a warrior's feast which is described.

Many of the banquets in David's palace must have been of this type. One of the features of his reign was that, like our own King Arthur with his knights of the Round Table, he collected round himself from all parts of the land the young men of promise and aspiration, and trained them up in valour

and usefulness. Their exploits were long
remembered by their countrymen with pride
and affection. At their head were the three
mighties, and after these the thirty; Joab
and Abishai, Benaiah and Asahel were names
familiar for generations afterwards as house-
hold words. These David sent forth to
clear the land of enemies and to widen its
borders on every hand; and, when they
came home to record their triumphs, no
doubt he feasted them in the palace, making
them feel how much he, rejoiced in their
valour and their victories.

3. AN IMAGE OF FRIENDSHIP.

Another element of the spiritual life imperfectly expressed by the image of the sheep
and the shepherd, but far more adequately
set forth by that of entertainer and guest,
is communion.

Between sheep and shepherd there is a
strong tie : they understand each other, and
may be said to love each other. Yet they
are far apart : between a brute and a man

there is a great gulf fixed. It may be said
that the gulf between man and God is wider
still. But this is not the case. The Eighth
Psalm boldly declares, in the correct translation
of the Revised Version, that man has been
made but a little lower than God; and all
Scripture unites in declaring that man was
made in the image of God. Man is capable
of knowing, loving and obeying his Creator,
and this is his highest honour. It is, indeed,
an infinite condescension on the part of God;
but He allows and invites man to a far closer
fellowship with Himself than it is possible
for a sheep to have with a man; and this
was the fact of religion which required to be
represented through a new image.

A banquet is a living image of fellowship.
To invite a man to be your guest is an
expression of respect and affection; and it
is an intimation that you wish to know more
of him, and to come closer to him. The
house is adorned, the table is spread with
unusual care, and the viands are chosen to
give him pleasure and do him honour. As
the feast proceeds, distance and shyness are

broken down ; the lips are opened, and the heart is opened. The host not only gives his entertainment, but he gives himself ; and the guest gives himself in return.

This is an image of religion. Religion is fellowship with God ; this is its very soul and essence. To be religious is to walk with God. It is to move all day long in an atmosphere warmed and enlightened by His presence. It is to realise Him to be so near that you can appeal to Him in every emergency, seek His aid in every time of need, and in every joy make Him your confidant. It is to see Him everywhere—in the sunshine, in the beauty of hill and dale, in the life of the market-place and the vicissitudes of home. This immensely brightens and intensifies life ; and in this sense all a Christian's life may be said to be a banquet. Others, sitting at the table of Providence, receive ordinary fare ; but those who enjoy God in everything partake of festal food. A crust, if God's blessing is given with it, and if it is received with thankfulness, causes more enjoyment than the most savoury food where God is forgotten. To the mind which can discern God the whole world becomes a king's palace.

But in another sense the Christian life may be compared to a banquet : not only is God in every part of it, but now and then He favours the soul with special seasons of communion. In its very nature a feast is an occasional thing : it does not take place every day. And perhaps, therefore, the experience for which it stands is one which is not the Christian's daily portion, but given as a special favour and reward now and then. There are such seasons : religion has not only its ordinary tenor, but its exceptional experiences—its mounts of transfiguration and its evenings in the upper room. At such times God comes very near, and fellowship is very close. Of such occurrences the saints of every age have spoken. Says one :

> Upon my heart, bestowed by Thee,
>   More gladness I have found
> Than they, even then when corn and wine
>   Did most with them abound.

The Royal Entertainer

Another, on the evening of a day spent in communion, said, "I had rather be a door-keeper in the house of my God than dwell in the tents of wickedness." St. Paul was caught up to the third heavens, and did not know whether he was in the body or out of the body. Read the *Confessions of St. Augustine*, or the *Sermons of St. Bernard*, Bunyan's *Grace Abounding*, or Rutherford's *Letters*, and you will see that the Christian life has what Bunyan calls its "golden hours"; and what makes these golden is the nearness of God and the sense of the divine love. Ordinary humanity no doubt has its rare and memorable moments too: it is a poor life in which there are not some days which shine like gold and diamonds among the wood, hay and stubble of ordinary experience—days so precious that they would not be exchanged for years of commonplace existence—but nothing earthly can lift the human spirit to such heights as the influence of the Spirit of God.

Perhaps I ought to interpret in detail the

The Psalm of Psalms

different parts of the banquet as they are described in the text—the food, which is no doubt chiefly intended in the opening words, "Thou preparest a table before me"; then the delightful extravagance of oil, with its cool touch, so grateful in an Eastern climate, and its fragrance, enveloping the senses; then the drink, so abundant as to overflow the wine-cup. In Christian experience something could easily be found corresponding to each of these; and those so disposed may exercise their ingenuity in finding it out. But I will not take the trouble; these are only poetical amplifications of the idea of a right regal banquet. The most important thing is that which underlies them without being expressed. What is the reason why you go to anyone's table when you are invited? It is not because you will get a better meal than you would at home, though this may be welcome; it is not for the abundance and the splendour, though you may feel these to be in place: it is friendship which takes you there; you go to find your friend, not to receive his food;

The Royal Entertainer

these externals are only preparations and
contributions to the true feast. So, in religion, it is God Himself we seek; and the
various blessings of salvation are nothing
in themselves except as they bring us nigh
to Him.

FOREVER

FOREVER

"Surely goodness and mercy shall follow me all the
days of my life:
And I will dwell in the house of the Lord forever."

ON a celebrated occasion King David, in
thanking God for the singular success which
had marked his life-history, made special
mention of the fact that God had pledged
to him His goodness for a great while to
come: "Then went King David in and sat
before the Lord, and he said, Who am I, O
Lord God, and what is my house, that Thou
hast brought me hitherto? And this was
yet a small thing in Thy sight, O Lord
God; but Thou hast spoken of Thy
servant's house for a great while to come.
And is this the manner of man, O Lord
God?"

The Psalm of Psalms

It is a wonderful mercy to be able not only to remember the past with gratitude, but to contemplate the future with confidence. Mortals are naturally terrified at the future. However bright the past may have been, the dread haunts them that in the future may be hiding some ironical revenge. After the foaming cup of life has been drunk, there may be bitter dregs at the bottom. We cannot tell what a day may bring forth. Only a step in front of every one of us hangs a dark curtain, which we cannot lift. Who knows what may be awaiting us in any of the unknown days of a new year?. It may be some spectre of misfortune, which will turn all our bright life into darkness. So whispers our ignorance.

Nor is the fear of the future always so vague. Some know that it must contain exceptional trials for them. The young man who has just come to the city to push his fortune finds himself confronted with danger at every turn. All the influences which have hitherto supported and en-

couraged him are left behind; he is surrounded with new temptations; the pace of
life is so fast that he has no time to think,
and the numbers and the novelty bewilder
him. He asks anxiously how he is to
survive the trying time, and whether it is
possible to come out with safety and honour
on the other side.

Many who have long survived this initial
stage yet fear the future, and not without
good cause. They have passed the summit
of life, and see before them the downward
slope on what is called the sunless side
of the hill. They must look forward to a
more limited range of activity, to failing
powers and to the infirmities of old age.
Must the sweetness of life, then, be only
a reminiscence of the past? So the world
believes:

> Gather the rosebuds while ye may,
> Old Time is still a-flying;
> And that same flower which blooms today
> Tomorrow will be dying.

Such is the philosophy of the world. But is
there a truer philosophy? is there a gospel

The Psalm of Psalms

which can assure us that the best is still in front—that the sun of life is not sinking behind our backs, but rising in the direction to which our faces are turned?

It is this blessed gospel which is embodied in the text. This Twenty-third Psalm, as we have seen, celebrates the past—it is a record of varied past experience—but it also speaks of the future " for a great while to come."

1. The Future on this Side of Death.

The sacred poet does not assume that the future will contain no difficulties or perils for him. On the contrary, he knows that his life is to be one of service and warfare. It is the same person we have speaking in this last verse who, in verse 5, described himself as seated at the table of the king, anointed with oil and drinking an overflowing cup. But, as we saw, that was a warrior, and the banquet was a reward for deeds bravely done. When, however, the feast is over, the soldier must gird on his armour again and return to the field. Enemies have been vanquished, but not the whole of them; there are still battles to fight and victories to win.

If we are in the army of God and know what it is to be rewarded by communion with Himself for past services, we must not grow weary in well-doing. There remains yet very much land to be possessed. God does not call us to a valetudinarian and cloistered virtue. He desires us to perform our part in the struggle of life, and in the common business of the world to play the man for Him. Besides, there is the burden of His cause to be borne, and the means have to be provided for extending His reign. The earth is the Lord's and must not be surrendered to the devil. Every department of human effort is yet to be holiness to the Lord; every corner of the globe is to be filled with His glory; every tribe of the human race to be numbered among His people. Every false form of faith must be exploded; every practice of cruelty and oppression by which the world is cursed must come to an end. The struggle

The Psalm of Psalms

is a long one; it is full of labour and peril; no Christian, however, dare decline it; to his dying day he must be a soldier.

But, as he leaves the banqueting house, to return to the field of action, who are these two figures that accompany him by order of the king? "Goodness and Mercy shall follow me all the days of my life." These two divine attributes are here personified: they are servants appointed to follow the departing guest, to see that no evil befalls him; they are guardian angels sent to protect him from calamity. In the Homeric poems gods and goddesses sometimes descend to the earth and visit the field of battle, to assist their favourites. In a moment of deadly peril a goddess will diffuse round the warrior who is too severely pressed a mist, in which he is removed from the sight of his foes; or, assuming human shape, a god will plunge into the struggle in which the mortal in whom he is interested is being worsted and, with a spear before whose point everything goes down, completely turn the tide of battle.

Forever

No such mythology finds admission into the sacred Scriptures ; but this is something like the function here intended for the personified Goodness and Mercy.

What attractive figures these two are— how full of sympathy and bounty ! Can there be any misfortune for which divine Goodness cannot find a remedy ? How can life ever become bare and empty when this kind angel is present, ready to pour in strength from the horn of plenty ? Still more welcome is Mercy ; ah, we cannot afford to be without her. Of all the dangers which the future contains, our chief fear is the danger arising from ourselves. The battle, however severe, would be nothing, if only we were absolutely sure of our own loyalty. But we have in us an evil heart of unbelief, which departs from the living God ; the old man within us would betray the whole cause to the enemy ; terrible is the force of besetting sin, frequent are our fits of coldness and backsliding. We require mercy every day.

But goodness and mercy shall follow us

The Psalm of Psalms

all the days of our life. In days of prosperity they will be with us, lest pride should betray us; in days of adversity, lest fear should make us turn back. It is true we can never tell with what a portent any new day may be in travail; but, let it be what it may, yet, if Goodness and Mercy be with us, what need we fear? In the hot days of youth and in the feeble days of old age; in the busy day of action, in the sequestered day of thought, and in the holiday of repose still they will be with us. As we sleep, they will keep watch and ward; and, when we awake, they will be ready to accompany us. In the day when friends are many they will be there, the best friends of all; and in the day when all have deserted us they will be there, never leaving or forsaking us. Finally, on the day of death, when the world is fading from our grasp, and around us are crowding the new shapes of the world unknown, still these old and familiar figures will be with us—" Goodness and Mercy shall follow me all the days of my life."

Forever

2. THE FUTURE ON THE OTHER SIDE OF DEATH.

The "great while to come," for which David had received the assurance of the Divine countenance, did not merely reach to the very end of this earthly life but extended beyond the boundary of death—"and I will dwell in the house of the Lord forever."

"The house of the Lord" is a common phrase for the temple or the tabernacle; and many have so understood it here. In this sense the text would mean that David would always have free access to God in His earthly house; and, of course, "forever" might not mean more than as long as he should live.

But "the house of the Lord" is not here intended in an ecclesiastical sense. It is the palace of the Divine King—the same in which the banquet of verse 5 took place. As a reward for his exploits the warrior was admitted once into the palace as a guest; the banquet being over, he had to return again to the field of battle; but he looked forward to a time when, all his battles being finished,

The Psalm of Psalms

he would be invited back to the palace, not again to enjoy a banquet lasting only for a night, but to be a permanent inmate of the place; as Mephibosheth was fed every day at King David's table.

The figurative language being stripped away, this looks as if it were the expression of an assurance that, after the efforts of the mortal life are over, those who love God will dwell forever in communion with Him in heaven.

To us there is nothing in the least novel in such an idea; but it is very unusual in the Old Testament — so unusual that many scholars would declare that it cannot possibly be supposed to have a place in one of the Psalms, especially if this be by David. One of the most extraordinary features of the Old Testament is the absence from it of the scenery of the future world to which in the New Testament we are accustomed. In the Books of Moses, for example, when the punishments are described which will ensue upon disobedience, all kinds of woes which can be endured in this world are piled up

in the most appalling numbers, but no
mention is made of punishment in a future
state of existence; and, in the same way,
when the rewards are mentioned which are
promised to obedience, all earthly blessings,
such as long life, plentiful harvests, political
peace and domestic joys, are enumerated, but
no mention is made of that which, according
to our notions, ought to be most prominent
of all—the promise of a reward in heaven
after death.

Not that the Hebrews supposed that at
death life is extinguished, and that there is no
existence beyond. Many things might be
adduced to prove that they were quite aware
that they would continue to exist. Thus
when anyone died, he was said to be
" gathered to his fathers "; that is, he went
to meet in the other world those who had
died before him ; and some passages appear
to show not only that there would be recog-
nition there, but that the inhabitants lived in
nations and tribes, as they had done in this
world. But the extraordinary thing is the
quality of the future life as they imagined it.

The Psalm of Psalms

The place where the dead assemble is called Sheol; and they often speak as if it were located somewhere below ground; but there is no clear description of it; and no wonder, for it is "the land of darkness and the shadow of death; a land of darkness, as darkness itself, without any order, and where the light is as darkness." Dim and shadowy, too, is the existence there : " there is no work, nor device, nor knowledge, nor wisdom in Sheol."

In such a prospect there was nothing to attract, but quite the reverse. Accordingly, the way in which even good men speak in the prospect of death is totally unlike what we should now expect in the mouth of a Christian. Read, for example, the prayer of Hezekiah, when he was sick and expected to die. There is not in it a scintillation of any bliss to which he was looking forward on the other side of death. On the contrary, he says, "I shall not see the Lord, even the Lord in the land of the living. Nothingness cannot praise Thee; death cannot celebrate Thee; they that go down into the pit cannot hope for Thy truth." Similarly in Psalm Thirty, a good man in prospect of death, but pleading hard for life, prays, " What profit is there in my blood when I go down to the pit? shall the dust praise Thee? shall it declare Thy truth?" And another psalmist pleads in similar circumstances, " For in death there is no remembrance of Thee; in the grave who shall give Thee thanks?" "The dead praise not the Lord," says another, "neither any that go down into silence." The Ecclesiast is the most doleful of all : " The living know that they must die; but the dead know not anything ; neither have they any more a reward; for the memory of them is forgotten. Also their love and their hatred and their envy is now perished; neither have they any more a portion forever in anything that is done under the sun."

What may have been the purpose of God in keeping the secret of the world to come hidden from so many of His servants, is an extremely interesting question. Perhaps it was because He wished them first to recognise that religion is a good thing for this life,

The Psalm of Psalms

apart altogether from a life to come. Certainly, when we read how the saints of the Old Testament rejoiced in God and declared that His love had made them happier than the godless ever could be, even when their corn and wine abounded, and when we reflect that these saints perhaps knew little or nothing about the rewards of the next life, we begin to suspect that perhaps their religious standpoint is not lower but higher than our own. Is our secret feeling not sometimes that the religious life in this world is a poor affair, the prizes and tit-bits falling mostly to the worldly and the wicked, but that what religion costs here will be compensated by the pleasures of the world to come? And, if this is our thought, were not those far above us who, apart altogether from the punishments and rewards coming afterwards, were confident that wickedness in all its forms is despicable and detestable, but that godliness is life and peace?

Another reason why the saints of the Old Testament were kept in the dark on this subject may have been that God does not

Forever

reveal the truth till it is needed. Truth given to those unprepared for it would have been little prized; but, when they were stretching out their hands and yearning with their whole hearts for it, then the revelation was seized with avidity and retained with tenacity.

In the Old Testament we see the human mind being prepared for the revelation of immortality, till at last it may be said to be panting for it, as the hart for water-brooks.

The need of it was felt in two ways. On the one hand, it was felt to be necessary, in order to make up for the imperfect justice of this life. The Mosaic Law taught that godliness and righteousness would have for reward prosperity in this world; and this was echoed in a hundred forms in the sacred books, as in the First Psalm, "Blessed is the man that walketh not in the counsel of the ungodly, nor standeth in the way of sinners, nor sitteth in the seat of the scornful. But his delight is in the law of the Lord, and in His law doth he meditate day and night. He shall be like a tree planted by the rivers of

water, that bringeth forth his fruit in his
season; his leaf also shall not wither; and
whatsoever he doeth shall prosper." But
although this principle, of prosperity attend-
ing the steps of the righteous, was amply
justified in the general course of history, it
was not justified in every case. Sometimes
the good man was not prosperous, and
sometimes the wicked were. In such cases
what was to be said? God's justice was not
vindicated in this life; must there not be
compensations in another life? Job was an
example of calamity after calamity falling on
a righteous man, and the whole Book of Job
may be said to consist of the moans and cries
of the human soul, as it knocked at the gate
of God for the revelation of immortality.

But the human spirit was also brought to
the same point along a happier path. Life,
according to Hebrew ideas, was the breath of
God: at the Creation God breathed into
man's nostrils the breath of life, and he
became a living soul; death, on the other
hand, is the withdrawal of the divine breath.
But, by living in constant intercourse with

Forever

God, might not the human being be so filled with the divine energy that he could not die? Sometimes the saints, when living very near to God, felt themselves to be so full of health and strength, derived from God Himself, that the conviction forced itself on their minds that nothing, not even temporal death, could separate them from His love. This is the glorious feeling of the Sixteenth Psalm:

I have set the Lord always before me:
Because He is at my right hand, I shall not be
    moved.
Therefore my heart is glad, and my glory rejoiceth:
My flesh also shall dwell in safety.
For Thou wilt not leave my soul to Sheol;
Neither wilt Thou suffer Thine holy one to see
    corruption.
Thou wilt shew me the path of life:
In Thy presence is fulness of joy;
At Thy right hand there are pleasures for evermore.

It was along this sunny path of communion with God that the singer of the Twenty-third Psalm also was led to belief; and, although his vision may have lasted only for a moment, it would be unwarrantable to deny that he may have seen the promised land.

The Psalm of Psalms

We, however, are more favourably situated. In the interval between the Old Testament and the New the mists in which the other life was enveloped began to clear away ; and the writers of the New Testament all adopted and developed the faith in immortality. Jesus Himself made the revelation of this hope peculiarly His own. He Himself breathed the atmosphere of the other world ; He raised the dead and was Himself raised from the dead ; He spoke of the many mansions in His Father's house ; and, as we follow His departing figure from the summit of Olivet, we obtain a very near view of that country in which those who have come to Him as the Shepherd and Bishop of their souls will be led to fountains of living water, and those who have worn themselves out in His service on earth will be made to rest from their labours forever.

APPENDIX

APPENDIX

THOUGH I have chosen, for title, THE PSALM OF PSALMS, other phrases may occur to the ingenious. Mr. Meyer has entitled his sweet and tender comment THE SHEPHERD PSALM, and Dr. John Stoughton called his THE SONG OF CHRIST'S FLOCK. A good title by an anonymous author is THE SHEPHERD KING; and an attractive one might be THE PSALM OF OUR CHILDHOOD.

When occupied with any portion of Scripture, I like to have at hand two commentaries —a thoroughly scientific one, to make clear what exactly the author said and intended, and a more devotional or homiletical one, to suggest applications. For the Psalms, the couple I have thus used most have been Hupfeld and Spurgeon.

Hupfeld is not only the best commentary on the Psalms known to me, but the best com-

Appendix

mentary I have ever used on any part of Scripture. In fact, it taught me what exegesis is. It is rationalistic; but it is easy to discount this; and nothing can surpass its learning and knowledge, its literary appreciation and intellectual grasp. Unfortunately it has not been translated; but much of the essence of it has been transferred to Perowne. Those who prefer what is more recent may turn to Kirkpatrick's three volumes, to be had bound in one, or Briggs' two volumes in the International Commentary.

As for Spurgeon's *Treasury of David*, the bulky volumes and miscellaneous contents will repel scholarly readers. Yet Spurgeon has far more learning than he gets credit for; he seldom misses the drift of a psalm; and in his heaps of accumulations there is many a remark or illustration that can be made to shine like a gem in a discourse. Maclaren's three volumes on the Psalms in the Expositor's Bible are among the best of his expository writings.

INDEX

I. QUOTATIONS

II. TOPICS

THE
SHORT COURSE SERIES

EDITED BY
Rev. JOHN ADAMS, B.D.

This Series is designed to encourage a healthy re-action in the direction of expository preaching. Leading expositors in all the Churches have kindly promised assistance; and the Series, to be issued at the uniform price of 60 cents net per volume, will furnish a sufficiently large variety for individual selection.

NOW READY

A CRY FOR JUSTICE: A Study in Amos.
By Prof. J. E. McFadyen, D.D., U. F. C. College, Glasgow.

THE BEATITUDES.
By Rev. Robert H. Fisher, D.D., Edinburgh.

THE LENTEN PSALMS.
By the Editor.

THE PSALM OF PSALMS.
By Prof. James Stalker, D.D., Aberdeen.

THE SONG AND THE SOIL.
By Prof. W. G. Jordan, D.D., Kingston, Ontario.

THE HIGHER POWERS OF THE SOUL.
By Rev. George M'Hardy, D.D., Kirkcaldy.

BELIEF AND LIFE: Expositions in the Fourth Gospel.
By Principal W. B. Selbie, D.D., Mansfield College, Oxford.

THE EMOTIONS OF JESUS.
By Prof. Robert Law, D.D., Toronto.

THE OVERTURES OF JESUS.
By Rev. Newell Dwight Hillis, D.D., Brooklyn.

IN THE UPPER ROOM.
By Rev. D. J. Burrill, D.D., LL.D., New York.

THE "I AM'S" OF OUR LORD.
By Rev. Thomas Marjoribanks, B.D., Edinburgh.

THE SEVEN WORDS FROM THE CROSS.
By Rev. A. B. Macaulay, M.A., Stirling.

THE PRAYERS OF ST. PAUL.
By Prof. W. G. Griffith Thomas, D.D., Toronto.

THE METAPHORS OF ST. PAUL.
By Rev. A. Boyd Scott, B.D., Glasgow.

THE HOLY SPIRIT.
By Rev. F. Stuart-Gardiner, B.D., Kingstown, Ireland.

THE REDEMPTION OF GOD.
By Prof. T. B. Kilpatrick, D.D., Toronto.

STUDIES IN THE APOCALYPSE.
By Prof. W. T. Davison, D.D., Richmond.

EXPOSITORY STUDIES.
By Prof. Arthur S. Péake, D.D., Manchester.

SOCIAL STUDIES.
By Rev. Canon Simpson, M.A., D.D., St. Paul's, London.

OPINIONS OF WEIGHT.

"I thank you very heartily for a copy of your 'Lenten Psalms.' Your 'Short Course Series' finds in this volume an interesting example of the kind of book you are proposing to produce. It is brightly written, and is full of stimulating illustration. I think it exceedingly likely the plan may meet a modern want. The Bible as a backbone for preaching appeals to people better than general sentiment or edifying exhortation of a vague type."

Bishop RYLE, D.D., Dean of Westminster.

"The book is attractive in a high degree, and nothing could be better calculated to stimulate expository preaching in the Churches. One may confidently anticipate for the Series a genuine success."

H. R. MACKINTOSH, D.D., Edinburgh.

"May I express my own judgment that you are working a very fruitful line, and that it will be most acceptable to a great many readers."

J. H. JOWETT, D.D., New York.

"I am wholly with you in this. And I wish you great success in what you are proposing to do. Your plan will help us all to give a scriptural breadth and fulness to our pulpit work. For this and other reasons I hail your proposal, and shall do all that I can to further your good work."

Principal ALEXANDER WHYTE, D.D., Edinburgh.

"You have got hold of a fine idea, and your Series, I am sure, will fulfil a most necessary ministry. There is vast need of just such expository preaching as you wish to encourage."

ALEXANDER SMELLIE, D.D., Carluke.